KU-207-350

THE STORY OF MY BOYHOOD AND YOUTH

John Muir (1838–1914) was born and raised in Dunbar, East Lothian. When his family emigrated to Wisconsin in 1849, young John was brought up to hard labour on his father's homestead. Yet he found time for reading and ingenious inventions which gave him an early reputation for brilliance.

After attending the University of Wisconsin, Muir pursued his mechanical skills until an industrial accident nearly blinded him. He set out on an epic walk from Indiana to the Gulf of Mexico, keeping a journal as he went, later published in 1916 as *A Thousand Mile Walk to the Gulf*. In 1868 he went to the Sierra Nevada mountains and spent five years in the Yosemite valley, which influenced the rest of his life. Living rough, Muir studied geology and the plant and animal life around him. His journals from this period, *My First Summer in the Sierra*, were published in 1911. In subsequent years he produced innumerable articles and lectures from the journals of regular summer trips to the mountains of California, Washington, Oregon, and Alaska. Marriage in 1880 took Muir out of the wilderness for a spell, until the need for its preservation involved him in a major campaign for the General Grant, Sequoia and Yosemite national parks, which were finally established in 1890. In the next ten years he overcame opposition from big business to the establishment of still more National Forest parks throughout the country and was a founder member of the Sierra Club which took up the cause of wilderness protection.

The Muir Woods National Monument was established in California in 1908, and John Muir has been, honoured ever since as the 'father' of the modern environment movement.

John Muir

THE STORY OF
MY BOYHOOD AND YOUTH

Introduction by David M. Anderson

Happy Christmas Jannice and all the best for 2016

Jannie

BIRLINN

This edition published in 2006 by
Birlinn Limited
West Newington House
10 Newington Road
Edinburgh
EH9 1QS

www.birlinn.co.uk

Reprinted 2013

First published in 1913 by Houghton Miflin Co.
Introduction copyright © David M. Anderson 2006

All rights reserved.
No part of this publication may be reproduced, stored
or transmitted in any form without the express written
permission of the publisher.

ISBN 978 1 78027 127 9

British Library Cataloguing-in-Publication Data
A catalogue record for this book is available from the British Library

Typeset by Iolaire Typesetting, Newtonmore
Printed and bound by Grafica Veneta
www.graficaveneta.com

CONTENTS

LIST OF ILLUSTRATIONS

INTRODUCTION

Scotland has sent so many people out into the world. For centuries they have gone, to fight others' wars, to build empires, to trade, to explore and to settle. They are going still. At one time, those left behind could only wonder at the experiences and fates of those who went overseas. Until comparatively recently communication was difficult and many emigrants never returned or were never heard from again. It has become easier in our technology rich world to keep in contact, to visit, and to experience other lands; but the tales of those who left in the past are often missing pages in Scotland's story. Sometimes, however, there is rediscovery. And long after he left his native town of Dunbar, more and more Scots are discovering the remarkable tale of John Muir, a man who, quite literally, changed the world.

This is Muir's first autobiographical work, although his Sierra journals were published before it appeared. Another 'chapter' in his life was edited and published posthumously. This book is very different from his campaigning articles and books although it was written with his life's work in mind. Although all too short it sets the scene for what was a lifetime of exploration and discovery. Writing as a son of Scotland, Muir recalls his beginnings and his family's transition to the brand new state of Wisconsin in the United States. He celebrates 'a never-failing source of wonder and delight' as new experiences piled into his consciousness. None of the hard, hard labour to which he was soon put appears to have inhibited his curiosity. His narrative overflows with examples of the effect the new world had on his senses. The tiredness of bone-aching farm-breaking did nothing to inhibit his determination to discover just how things worked – even if this meant outwitting his formidable father.

It is unfortunate, but typical of Muir, that he never completed more of his autobiography or even the accounts of his explorations. Completing them would indeed have been a daunting task if only because Muir's explorations and experiences are almost unmatched even in the annals of America. His travels took him to every continent and many times from California to the wilds of Alaska. But he hated the labour of writing for publication. He was only really at home in the woods and wilds; offices, hotels, towns and cities were alien environments to him. He felt that mere words on a sterile page could never do justice to his beloved wilderness: better, by far, he thought, for everyone to experience at least once 'a trip to the woods'. Once there his philosophy would speak for itself in the voice of the pure 'wildness' that would surround them. On the other hand, it is well recorded that in the right circumstances he could enthral audiences with his wilderness tales and inspire them with the necessary task of ensuring that future generations would have a chance of experiencing true wildness. The enthusiasm of his public speaking carried over into his private correspondence. Paradoxically, for a man who hated writing,he was a life-long letter writer.The fullest expression of his philosophy comes in the unfettered liberty he found in corresponding with his large circle of friends. The words would flow as they never did when he shut himself away to worry at the task of producing articles and essays for publication. Indeed, it is through letters that he first found his way into print – friends felt that his words to them were worthy of much wider circulation. Muir puzzled over this conundrum until he was dragooned into a partial solution.

It was only by an intervention by his friends that this work was even begun. During 1908 the railway magnate Edward Harriman cajoled Muir up to his isolated lodge at Klamath Lake. Providing a stenographer to capture Muir's narration, the poor author 'was fairly compelled to make a beginning': 'being kept so busy, dictating autobiographical stuff, I'm fair dizzy most of the time, and I can't get out of it, for there's no withstanding Harriman's stenographer under orders'. This horrible effort produced more that a thousand pages – still extant in manuscript and now microfilm. The narrated work is a plainer, franker, more revealing account that the published version. Despite this good start, it was all very well getting the words down on paper but then the old Muir took over and the text was worried over, edited, expanded or rejected several times over. Five more years passed before it appeared in book form. The result is, despite its frankness, heavily edited around family matters and childhood experiences. It was a bold step for anyone of Muir's time to be so revealing about domestic tyranny. Muir found himself on the defensive over some aspects of the work as it first appeared. Nonetheless, in a letter to a childhood friend preserved in the archives of Wisconsin Historical Society his brother Daniel wrote that John felt that 'he knew the old people were honest, sincere & meant all for the best, but he wanted to put his foot down hard on every thing that was harsh, cruel & unkind'. Many events described in the draft were omitted, wholly or in part, the core of what remained serving to illustrate those aspects of his upbringing and childhood that perhaps emphasised his 'wildness' over other considerations.

Thus, this volume sets the scene for a self-proclaimed life as 'a wandering wilderness lover' but this was Muir exhibiting Scottish self-effacement in the extreme. He was not by any calling a simple rustic savant. Although by appearance and occasional behaviour extremely eccentric, he was a shrewd businessman when he had to be, an original thinker, and was possessed of a steely determination. Some of these attributes are plain in this volume; others were exhibited later in life. In fact, his life included periods as technologist and tramp, botanist and naturalist, geologist and glaciologist, farmer and trader, family man and loner in the wilderness, mountaineer, writer, campaigner, visionary and philosopher. In many of these facets he shone, sometimes brilliantly, but on top of all these he was first and foremost one of the world's first practical and effective environmentalists, a champion of 'preservation'. He did much of his pioneering work on solo trips and could have become just another curious 'mountain man' of the Californian uplands. Nevertheless, the links with his many friends, the duty imposed by his Presbyterian upbringing, and the simple need to communicate his discoveries kept him in contact with civilisation. Pressure from his friends led to publication and publication led to reputation and increasing influence.

He was celebrated in his adopted land long before he died, where his hundreds of articles, his books, lectures and campaigning had won him a high profile; but at home, beyond a few family members, there was little awareness of his fame. It is true that a clutch of obituaries appeared following his death in 1914 but they give the impression of acknowledging his passing without understanding his significance. Indeed, even at the present time, close to a century after Muir died, his significance is still generally unappreciated in his home country, although his adopted land seems convinced.

This work does not touch on these later achievements although it is informed by them. It sets the scene for his life and covers the period from Muir's birth in 1838 and emigration in 1849 to leaving the family farm in 1860 and his four years at the University of Wisconsin.

It begins in Dunbar, then a prosperous Scottish town much like any other. Dunbar had had a long and at times bloody history, as recalled by John and his school friends when they re-enacted the battles of old and played in the ruins of the ancient sea-girt castle beside the brand new Victoria Harbour. The days of battle were long past and Dunbar flourished as the centre of a rich agricultural region. Its principal industries were geared towards its pastoral hinterland although a substantial part of the community earned a living from the sea. In John's time, the burgh and parish of Dunbar had a population of around 4,500, of whom two thirds lived in the town, then a compact community where most still lived within what had been the medieval boundaries. Burgh life centred on the broad

High Street and the closes or pends running off it. Between the High Street and the harbours was an area devoted to work-shops and maritime trades and the homes of the workers in these trades.Three nearby villages, a few hamlets and over a dozen large farms accounted for most of the remainder. Most of the farms belonged to one or other of several large land-holdings or estates but a few, usually those nearer the burgh, were in the hands of owner-occupiers, mostly merchants who had prospered in Dunbar itself. The community could rank itself from pauper to aristocrat, but the mass were labourers, artisans, shopkeepers and merchants who governed themselves by means of the town and parish councils.

Improvement had made the farms of East Lothian some of the best in Britain.Their peak harvest workforces could run to over 100 hands. Their output was mostly grain and potatoes, which grew well in the rich red soil. In these days most farms also reared livestock – cattle on the plain, sheep in the hills. They generated considerable wealth – many farmers had been shareholders in the East Lothian Bank. When the bank failed during the 1820s it left a six-figure debt (equivalent to a multi-million pound sum today), which was honoured in full by the shareholders.

Dunbar merchants profited from trading on the produce and supplying the needs of the farms and estates. A lot of the equipment they (and the fishing community) needed was made in Dunbar itself. The town still had a robust manufacturing sector, just one substantial component of a mixed economy. As an example, Sked's foundry, which employed as many hands (22 in 1841) as the three local breweries combined, had a reputation for producing reliable and efficient agricultural steam engines. Advertisements boast that the firm would 'warrant them to work satisfactorily, with very little more than one-half the fuel and water required for others'. A dozen or more were turned out yearly, mainly to drive threshing machines and other farm equipment. Other family businesses produced ropes and sails, harness and saddlery, and all the millwright and smith-work required; their workshops made and repaired carriages, carts and all manner of farm machinery from sophisticated reapers and binders down to the meanest hoe. Dunbar had a large malt trade, processing vast amounts of local and even imported barley for the brewing and distilling industries. John would have been exposed to much of this industry and it could be envisioned that he would have found employment there, had he stayed in Dunbar. His father and grandfather had many contacts with the farming sector. His playmates were the sons and daughters of the town's merchants and artisans.

Although doing well during Muir's boyhood, the town was beginning to face up to changes happening in the wider world. It benefited from two massive construction projects in the 1840s. The first was self initiated and the second was part of a national phenomenon. Dunbar had long felt the need for improved port facilities. Several schemes were floated and the eventual result was in 1842 the New or Victoria Harbour. Its construction was not without loss as a new channel was blasted through the Castle Rock – with the disappearance of much of the old castle ruins. Muir talked about the harbour works in his draft manuscript, but excised all references in this final book. The intention of the harbour development was to bolster the town's maritime trade, which had been declining due to the poor access and wharfage of the older harbour. The other major project showed that local schemes were now very much dependant upon national events. A station opened at Dunbar serving the new Edinburgh to Berwick railway line. In its first year of operation the herring trade switched almost exclusively to this new and fast network – rendering the recent harbour a near white elephant. Dunbar had lost the greater part of its locally registered merchant fleet by the time the Muirs left in 1849.

Both projects had necessitated an influx of labour, mainly Irish navvies, which caused some local stresses and excitement. Such tensions were dealt with by Dunbar town council, which was responsible for everything locally from policing to piggeries. When Muir was growing up, political reform of the previous decade was beginning to bear fruit.

As well as the major construction projects there was much occurring on a more modest scale. The town's leading citizens were beginning to invest in new buildings on the town's ancient High Street by replacing tenements of the eighteenth or earlier centuries or by building on new sites outside the historic boundaries of the town. Although stone from nearby quarries was preferred for much of this work, a large works at nearby West Barns manufactured a wide range of brick, tile and pipe work. Several limekilns just to the east of Dunbar supplied the building trades and agriculture (where lime served as an improver for clay soils). Progress was also underway in the provision of utilities and services – increased water supplies were secured and a local gas production company was floated.

When David Gilrye, John Muir's grandfather, was in his prime, he served a couple of terms (six years) as a councillor. In these days, a councillor could serve for life if one wished (or, more realistically, was able to keep in with the ruling clique). Election had degenerated to a form of nomination so a dominant faction need never relinquish power. Burgh reform was implemented in the 1830s. The town council opened up to a greater constituency with an extended franchise, the abolition of some restrictions on eligibility and even entitlement to vote. Remarkably, this tempted even Daniel Muir, John Muir's father, to get involved in secular affairs. Somebody, somehow, convinced him to give politics a go and he was able sufficiently to put aside his religious scruples to stand for office. Muir senior was elected for a three-year term at the end of 1847, standing down when he emigrated. Many positions on the board were still in the hands of the 'old guard' represented by Provost Simon Sawers of Newhouse, Bailie David France of Seafield, and former provost Christopher Middlemass of Underedge. Although each of these three was a landed proprietor, appearances were deceptive: Middlemass began as a clerk in a Dunbar merchant's office, before flourishing in business himself; France was a baker to trade who spotted a niche in cement and brick making; and Sawers came from a family with mercantile roots in nearby Haddington. All could be models

xvi The Story of My Boyhood and Youth

for the progress in position and wealth Muir senior was making during his time in Dunbar. Councillors John Kirkwood and James Miller junior were from old Dunbar families, but represented the flourishing shopkeepers of the burgh, and Robert Morton and John Richardson the professionals, being respectively a teacher and a retired naval purser. Most of the rest of the board followed the pattern thus set.

The reformed town council became more attentive to its electors and its duties as new people gained seats. It is possible that John's father was associated with a few other newcomers united by their active association in a dissenting congregation in the town: Muir's neighbour, Alex Cunningham, and Matthew Watt, who bought Muir's first Dunbar home in 1846, are in this category. Although at first sight a trivial association, the Secession church congregation had split from mainstream Presbyterianism over exactly the kind of thing that had corrupted the old civic system, namely restrictive practices, the swearing of burgess oaths and burgh or church patronage – where secular authority interfered with religious prerogatives. It looks like Daniel and his friends were liberated by reform in the 1830s and had the support in the 1840s to gain at least a few council seats.

As he aged, more and more of Daniel Muir's behaviour and indeed character was dictated to by his literal interpretation of his Bible, as his son makes clear. He had grown up as an orphan farm labourer in his elder sister's household on farms in Crawfordjohn parish in the Upper Ward of Lanarkshire. This old heartland of Covenanters and Cameronians still had a strongly evangelical character and Daniel Muir appears himself to have been converted to evangelical Presbyterianism around the age of 14. Once a promising fiddler and keen attendee of farms kirns, he put frivolity aside for good and all. He left home to seek his fortune, and after joining an unknown regiment of the British Army ended up in Dunbar with a roving commission as a recruiting sergeant. His military career went by the board when he married a Dunbar girl, although his first hopes of settling down were dashed when she died shortly afterwards. She left him in possession of a lease on a tenement and a shop on the High Street. In notices of the time he is recorded as a mealdealer – a seller of oatmeal. He built his business into a flourishing success and is later described as merchant, a sign of greatly improved local status. He was able to buy a large tenement and garden in 1841, a first step to satisfying his 'land hunger'. The property was one of the largest within the town and its possession was a statement in its own right. In an advertisement 1821 of it was described thus: 'That large and commodious house . . . with two good gardens, stables, and coachhouse. The house is well calculated for the accommodation of a genteel and numerous family, consisting of parlour, dining room, drawing room, and five excellent bedrooms, with a light bed closet to each of them, besides four garret rooms, kitchen and servant's room, cellars and other conveniences.' Daniel Muir must have taken some satisfaction at the progress he had made. Muir senior made also substantial donations to his church, and probably to other causes. It was not economic necessity that drove him to take his family to America.

There were many schools in Dunbar that Muir senior could have selected for his children's education. Primary (or elementary) education was a private matter in the burgh, although parish schools catered to the youth of the villages of East and West Barns. A charity school had recently been established for the young of the poorer part of the community but several private teachers had schools that catered to the youth of the middling classes. Thus, John's first schoolmaster was Mungo Suddon ('Siddons' in the text), who had rooms close to the Methodist Church on the Dawell Brae (now Victoria Street). Suddon's school took pupils from infancy to the age of 16 or 17 but it was more usual for children to transfer to the mathematical or grammar schools once they had a grounding in the 3Rs. This is the route that John took. At the grammar school he had to begin again with new classmates, lessons and masters and he vividly remembered these days when he was writing this book towards the end of his life. The grounding his

Scottish schooling gave him by the age of eleven was more than sufficient to enable him to hold his own later at university in Madison.

Just across the High Street from the family home was a tenement belonging to Muir's maternal grandparents. David Gilrye and his wife Margaret Hay were once also incomers to Dunbar. He was from Mindrum in Northumberland and she from Coldstream. They had prospered in Dunbar. Gilrye had been a flesher or butcher and was one of the town's respected burgesses. As well as his town council stint his commitment to the established church was reflected in long service as an elder. He crops up in the records of the time as witness in civic and legal transactions and was often approached to act as a surety for prospective licensees.

The Gilryes' lives had been touched by tragedy – eight of their ten children had died young and one of their remaining daughters had lost her husband at an early age as well as two of her three children. There might then been questions over Ann's choice of a husband: a seeming rootless soldier who was most definitely not in communion with the established church. When Daniel Muir uprooted his family to chase his religious dreams the Gilryes' remaining solace (their brood of grand-children) appeared to be vanishing for good. However, it is clear that Gilrye respected Daniel Muir's business sense, if not his religious convictions. Muir senior was written in as a prospective trustee to Gilrye's estate and was given his second son David Gilrye Muir's small inheritance to manage until the boy came of age.

The children were probably shielded from family arguments about religion – Muir makes no reference to them – but they felt the full force of Daniel's passion at home. Perhaps to compensate, their grandparents' fireside became a favourite evening refuge for the children. It was probably there that Muir's lifelong love of Scottish tales, poetry and romance was kindled. And it was at that fireside that the awesome news was broken on one February evening – they were going to America the very next morning.

The children had but a single day's notice, although Muir senior must have been planning the trip for some time. The house was sold, the tickets were bought, a fearsome amount of goods ('our formidable load of stuff') was purchased for the new life, and it had been agreed that an advance party would go first and welcome Muir's mother and younger siblings once they were set up. The exact destination, however, was rather nebulous.

All his time in Dunbar Muir senior had been chaffing at the restrictions of British life.Secular and religious rules and regulations prevented him from fully following his dream, which by the time of departure had become to follow a fully-fledged life of Biblical literalism. One sect in particular had caught his attention. The Body of the Disciples in Christ (or simply, Disciples of Christ) promised that in the New World a New Jerusalem might be attained. At least one of their itinerant preacher-recruiters had Dunbar links and Muir senior thought he had found his answer; his family appears to have little say in the decision.The Disciples had several colonies in Canada and the States and it was for one of these that the family headed.

To John Muir it was the first big adventure of his life, setting the pattern he followed ever after. Their voyage, 'six weeks and three days', was Muir's first experience of real freedom as he immersed himself in the workings of the ship. As he writes, it got even better when they had landed and had made their way to the hamlet of Kingston, Wisconsin, as Muir senior was soon absent prospecting a good site for a farmstead. It is perhaps a sign of Muir senior's disillusionment with his old country that at about then he found time to appear before a notary and renounce his British citizenship and become an American; his son waited another 50 years before he felt the need! But once the land was secured the 'hard, hard work' feared by his grandfather began. The Muirs secured a plot with both creek and lake with prairie, oak woods and clearings. Muir senior was no farmer, despite his rural upbringing. The proportion of arable in Crawfordjohn was tiny in comparison to the extent devoted to sheep farming and his relatives had been shepherds

– employed on the land but not making the decisions. His experience in East Lothian was in buying and selling grain and meal – again, at a remove from real husbandry. His abiding interest was religion and he was soon often absent as he debated and preached in the community; the children were left with all tasks of the farm under Muir senior's 'generalship'.

In The Heart of John Muir's World, Millie Stanley delves into Muir's Wisconsin days. Stanley picks the strength of family ties they exhibited as being of key importance in Muir's later career – despite his seeming love of loneliness and the wilderness. She also picks out the stories still circulating around the neighbourhood of Fountain Lake and Hickory Hill farms about the discipline inflicted on his children by Daniel Muir. He was not alone. In this brand new state, in a brand new township, many of the settlers in the area cleaved to the same passions as Muir senior. Some interpreted severity as the route towards salvation. As anywhere there was a spectrum of opinion; some were more tolerant, allowed more. Although many of the community were Scots, they were from many different places – Edinburgh, Fife, Lanarkshire (Muir senior's home county) and more. They all brought a wealth of experience – miners, foresters, farmers and these trades found in more urban environments – that naturally found a way into being shared. When Muir passed out during the digging of a well, Willie Duncan, who learnt his stonecraft in Lanarkshire, was on hand to pass on the tricks of the trade and show the Muirs how to test for bad air and provide good. Although a good proportion of these neighbours shared some connection with the Disciples, each was open to their own interpretation of the sect's teaching. So although Muir senior felt no need for books bar the Bible others had brought good libraries. The Scots in Buffalo Township brought their tales and traditions too. Muir absorbed as much as he could and found like-minded friends and neighbours with whom to exchange or loan books or join together is some after-work activity such as singing schools.

In bringing both farms into cultivation, Muir gained a first-hand education into the processes that had created the landscape around Dunbar back home in Scotland where everything was owned by someone and put to some productive use. He came to the land as it was wild, a frontier at the very edge of civilisation, and through his own labour the settlements, fields and roads were spread and the borders of the wilderness were pushed back leaving only a few pockets behind. By the time he left home he had already formed ideas about preserving untouched some places that had been particularly dear to him. Several times he asked his brother to set aside a particular patch of lake-side meadow. The destructive effect man could have on the wilderness was reinforced when he finally reached the west coast a few years after leaving home. Near Yosemite he worked as a sheepherder and saw the havoc they wreaked on the upland meadows and how the indiscriminate practices of lumbermen were destroying in a few short years forests that had taken millennia to reach their majesty. This triple experience of civilisation's spread helped to formulate his life's work.

Autobiography generally is understood to have a factual basis. Many of the people and events that Muir discusses can be checked against contemporary records. Father, grandfather, and others he names all left traces. His first schoolmaster, Dominie Mungo Suddon, held several official and secretarial positions in Dunbar besides being a schoolmaster – remarkably, his name persisted in the so-called 'Siddon's Society' (or the Dunbar Mutual Assistance and Savings Society) until the 1990s. Even his childhood friends Bob Richardson, the son of a retired naval purser and Dunbar's town chamberlain, or Willie Chisholm, son of a butler in West Barns, can be found.

Sometimes an event he recounts reveals the child's perspective. When he describes finding apples bobbing in the surf after a wreck perhaps an adult would have recalled more grizzly fruit from that tide. As well as Le Rodeur, from Bruges for Glasgow with apples, four others ships were cast ashore around Dunbar with the loss of a dozen lives on a single night. Even the apples and figs he had from Lord Lauderdale's gardener hide the fact that gardener George Brown's daughter had married a distant cousin of Muir during 1844.

Much of the rest of the descriptions of family life can be corroborated by comments from his brothers and sisters that have survived, such as that noted above, or by evidence gleaned by Millie Stanley on Wisconsin days.

When this book was being prepared for its first publication in 1913, Muir intended that some 'good photographs' of his old Dunbar haunts should be included. However, it appeared with only one – a photograph of his childhood home. Muir had failed to find the required pictures in time, because his plan was derailed by the death of an intermediary. However, word eventually got through. From Dunbar, photographer Thomas Bisset wrote to Muir beginning during 1914 a correspondence that continued to within months of Muir's death. Bisset sent a good number of Dunbar views, going to some trouble to source an 'old' view of Muir's school (subsumed within extensions built in 1878 and in the 1890s). Other themes included the church and kirkyard where his relatives rested, the fishing quarter in Dunbar, and some of the nearby sights – the playgrounds of Muir's youth. Muir sent Bisset copies of his books in return and the two discussed both Dunbar and Muir's reminiscences.

Bisset's photographs remained in the possession of the Muir family and ultimately found their way into the John Muir Papers held at the Department of Special Collections of the Holt-Atherton Library of the University of the Pacific in California. Some have been include in this volume for the first time.

Muir's legacy, prescience, and significance are increasingly recognised. The Sierra Club, of which he was founding and life president, has grown in strength and authority over the past century. His old house in Martinez, California, where much of his writing and campaigning was based,was created a national monument in 1964.That campaign coincided with rediscovery in Scotland when Muir enthusiasts came to Dunbar seeking their hero's roots, to discover what made the man tick. In turn, they inspired local enthusiasm. John Muir Country Park was named in his honour in 1976 and covers much of the coast to the west of Dunbar where he used to play by the 'stormy North Sea'. A small museum was created in his birthplace during 1980, which reopened in 2003 after investment, renovation and reinterpretation. Dunbar's John Muir Association was formed in 1993 and helps to interpret his message in East Lothian. On the national scene, the John Muir Trust was formed in 1983 and now holds in stewardship several large tracts of wild land, which it manages on sustainable principles with local communities. Its John Muir award is increasingly popular and enables anyone to get to grips with studying and conserving their own patch of wild, small or big.

Animals and plants have been named in his honour; schools, streets, institutions and more bear his name. All over the world national parks owe some thanks to the pioneering campaign that he and his allies fought at the end of the nineteenth century. Now even Scotland has its own national parks! To many admirers his legacy is intangible – an idea or feeling or spirit, perhaps a journey one can make himself or herself – inspired by the body of work he has left behind, much of which has never been out of print.

This book tells how it all began.

David M. Anderson
May 2006.

Chapter 1

A BOYHOOD IN SCOTLAND

When I was a boy in Scotland I was fond of everything that was wild, and all my life I've been growing fonder and fonder of wild places and wild creatures. Fortunately around my native town of Dunbar, by the stormy North Sea, there was no lack of wildness, though most of the land lay in smooth cultivation. With red-blooded playmates, wild as myself, I loved to wander in the fields to hear the birds sing, and along the seashore to gaze and wonder at the shells and seaweeds, eels and crabs in the pools among the rocks when the tide was low; and best of all to watch the waves in awful storms thundering on the black headlands and craggy ruins of the old Dunbar Castle when the sea and the sky, the waves and the clouds, were mingled together as one. We never thought of playing truant, but after I was five or six years old I ran away to the seashore or the fields most every Saturday, and every day in the school vacations except Sundays, though solemnly warned that I must play at home in the garden and back yard, lest I should learn to think bad thoughts and say bad words. All in vain. In spite of the sure sore punishments that followed like shadows, the natural inherited wildness in our blood ran true on its glorious course as invincible and unstoppable as stars.

My earliest recollections of the country were gained on short walks with my grandfather when I was perhaps not over three years old. On one of these walks Grandfather took me to Lord Lauderdale's gardens, where I saw figs growing against a sunny wall and tasted some of them, and got as many apples to eat as I wished. On another memorable walk in a hayfield, when we sat down to rest on one of the haycocks I heard a sharp, prickly, stinging cry, and, jumping up eagerly, called Grandfather's attention to it. He said he heard only the wind, but I insisted on digging into the hay and turning it over until we discovered the source of the strange exciting sound – a mother field mouse with half a dozen naked young hanging to her teats. This to me was a wonderful discovery. No hunter could have been more excited on discovering a bear and her cubs in a wilderness den.

I was sent to school before I had completed my third year. The first schoolday was doubtless full of wonders, but I am not able to recall any of them. I remember the servant washing my face and getting soap in my eyes, and Mother hanging a little green bag with my first book in it around my neck so I would not lose it, and its blowing back in the sea-wind like a flag. But before I was sent to school my grandfather, as I was told, had taught me my letters from shop signs across the street. I can remember distinctly how proud I was when I had spelled my way through the little first book into the second, which seemed large and important, and so on to the third. Going from one book to another formed a grand triumphal advancement, the memories of which still stand out in clear relief.

The third book contained interesting stories as well as plain reading and spelling lessons. To me the best story of all was 'Llewellyn's Dog,' the first animal that comes to mind after the needle-voiced field mouse. It so deeply interested and touched me and some of my classmates that we read it over and over with aching hearts, both in and out of school, and shed bitter tears over the brave faithful dog, Gelert, slain by his own master, who imagined that he had devoured his son because he came to him all bloody when the boy was lost, though he had saved the child's life by killing a big wolf. We have to look far back to learn how great may be the capacity of a child's heart for sorrow and sympathy with animals as well as with human friends and neighbors. This auld-lang-syne story stands out in the throng of old schoolday memories as clearly as if I had myself been one of that Welsh hunting-party – heard the bugles blowing, seen Gelert slain, joined in the search for the lost child, discovered it at last happy and smiling among the grass and bushes beside the dead, angled wolf, and wept with Llewellyn over the sad fate of his noble, faithful dog friend.

Another favorite in this book was Southey's poem 'The Inchcape Bell,' a story of a priest and a pirate. A good priest in order to warn seamen in dark stormy weather hung a big bell on the dangerous Inchcape Rock. The greater the storm and higher the waves, the louder rang the warning bell, until it was cut off and sunk by wicked Ralph the Rover. One fine day, as the story goes, when the bell was raging gently, the pirate put out to the rock, saying, 'I'll Sink that bell and plague the Abbot of Aberbrothok.' So he cut the rope, and down went the bell 'with a gurgling sound; the bubbles rose and burst around,' etc. Then 'Ralph the Rover sailed away; he scoured the seas for many a day; and now, grown rich with plundered store, he steers his course for Scotland's shore.' Then came a terrible storm with cloud darkness and night darkness and high roaring waves. 'Now where we are,' cried the pirate, 'I cannot tell, but I wish I could hear the Inchcape bell.' And the story goes on to tell how the wretched rover 'tore his hair,' and curst himself in his despair,' when 'with a shivering shock' the stout ship struck on the Inchcape Rock, and went down with Ralph and his plunder beside the good priest's bell. The story appealed to our love of kind deeds and of wildness and fair play.

A lot of terrifying experiences connected with these first schooldays grew out of crimes committed by the keeper of a low lodging-house in Edinburgh, who allowed poor homeless wretches to sleep on benches or the floor for a penny or so a night, and, when kind Death came to their relief, sold the bodies for dissection to Dr Hare of the medical school. None of us children ever heard anything like the original story. The servant girls told us that 'Dandy Doctors,' clad in long black cloaks and supplied with a store of sticking-plaster of won-drous adhesiveness, prowled at night about the country lanes and even the tow streets, watching for children to choke and sell. The Dandy Doctor's business method, as the servants explained it, was with lightning quickness to clap a sticking-plaster on the face of a scholar, covering mouth and nose, preventing breathing or crying for help, then pop us under his long black cloak and carry us to Edinburgh to be sold and sliced into small pieces for folk to learn how we were made. We always mentioned the name 'Dandy Doctor' in a fearful whisper, and never dared venture out of doors after dark. In the short winter days it got dark before school closed, and in cloudy weather we sometimes had difficulty in finding our way home unless a servant with a lantern was sent for us; but during the Dandy Doctor period the school was closed earlier, for if detained until the usual hour the teacher could not get us to leave the schoolroom. We would rather stay all night supperless than dare the mysterious doctors supposed to be lying in wait for us. We had to go up a hill called the Davel Brae that lay between the schoolhouse and the main street. One evening just before dark, as we were running up the hill, one of the boys shouted, 'A Dandy Doctor! A Dandy Doctor!' and we all fled pellmell back into the school-house to the astonishment of Mungo Siddons, the teacher. I can remember to this day the amused look on the good dominie's face as he stared and tried to guess what had got into us, until one of the older boys breathlessly explained that there was an awful big Dandy Doctor on the Brae and we couldna gang hame. Others corroborated the dreadful news. 'Yes! We saw him, plain as onything, with his lang black cloak to hide us in, and some of us thought we saw a sticken-plaister ready in his hand.' We were in such a state of fear and trembling that the teacher saw he wasn't going to get rid of us without going himself as leader. He went only a short distance, however, and turned us over to the care of the two biggest scholars, who led us to the top of the Brae and then left us to scurry home and dash into the door like pursued squirrels diving into their holes.

Just before school skaled (closed), we all arose and sang the fine hymn 'Lord, dismiss us with Thy blessing.' In the spring

when the swallows were coming back from their winter homes
we sang –

> Welcome, welcome, little stranger,
> Welcome from a foreign shore:
> Safe escaped from many a danger . . .

– and while singing we all swayed in rhythm with the music.
'The Cuckoo,' that always told his none in the spring of the
year, was another favorite song, and when there was nothing
in particular to call to mind any special bird or animal, the
songs we sang were widely varied, such as –

> The whale, the beast for me,
> Plunging along through the deep, deep sea.

But the best of all was 'Lord, dismiss us with Thy blessing,'
though at that time the most significant part I fear was the first
three words.

With my school lessons Father made me learn hymns and
Bible verses. For learning 'Rock of Ages' he gave me a penny,
and I thus became suddenly rich. Scotch boys are seldom
spoiled with money. We thought more of a penny those
economical days than the poorest American schoolboy thinks
of a dollar. To decide what to do with that first penny was an
extravagantly serious affair. I ran in great excitement up and
down the street, examining the tempting goodies in the shop
windows before venturing on so important an investment. My
playmates also became excited when the wonderful news got
abroad that Johnnie Muir had a penny, hoping to obtain a
taste of the orange, apple, or candy it was likely to bring forth.

At this time infants were baptized and vaccinated a few days
after birth. I remember very well a fight with the doctor when
my brother David was vaccinated. This happened, I think,
before I was sent to school. I couldn't imagine what the doctor,
a tall, severe-looking man in black, was doing to my brother,
but as Mother, who was holding him in her arms, offered no

objection, I looked on quietly while he scratched the arm until I saw blood. Then, unable to trust even my mother, I managed to spring up high enough to grab and bite the doctor's arm, yelling that I wasna gan to let him hurt my bonnie brither, while to my utter astonishment Mother and the doctor only laughed at me. So far from complete at times is sympathy between parents and children, and so much like wild beasts are baby boys, little fighting, biting, climbing pagans.

Father was proud of his garden and seemed always to be trying to make it as much like Eden as possible, and in a corner of it he gave each of us a little bit of ground for our very own, in which we planted what we best liked, wondering how the hard dry seeds could change into soft leaves and flowers and find their way out to the light; and, to see how they were coming on, we used to dig up the larger ones, such as peas and beans, every day. My aunt had a corner assigned to her in our garden, which she filled with lilies, and we all looked with the utmost respect and admiration at that precious lily-bed and wondered whether when we grew up we should ever be rich enough to own anything like so grand. We imagined that each lily was worth an enormous sum of money and never dared to touch a single leaf or petal of them. We really stood in awe of them. Far, far was I then from the wild lily gardens of California that I was destined to see in their glory.

When I was a little boy at Mungo Siddons's school a flower-show was held in Dunbar, and I saw a number of the exhibitors carrying large handfuls of dahlias, the first I had ever seen. I thought them marvelous in size and beauty and, as in the case of my aunt's lilies, wondered if I should ever be rich enough to own some of them.

Although I never dared to touch my aunt's sacred lilies, I have good cause to remember stealing some common flowers from an apothecary, Peter Lawson, who also answered the purpose of a regular physician to most of the poor people of the town and adjacent country. He had a pony which was considered very wild and dangerous, and when he was called out of town he mounted this wonderful beast, which, after standing long in the stable, was frisky and boisterous, and often to our delight reared and jumped and danced about from side to side of the street before he could be persuaded to go ahead. We boys gazed in awful admiration and wondered how the druggist could be so brave and able as to get on and stay on that wild beast's back. This famous Peter loved flowers and had a fine garden surrounded by an iron fence, through the bars of which, when I thought no one saw me, I oftentimes snatched a flower and took to my heels. One day Peter discovered me in this mischief, dashed out into the street and caught me. I screamed that I wouldna steal any more if he would let me go. He didn't say anything but just dragged me along to the stable where he kept the wild pony, pushed me in right back of its heels, and shut the door. I was screaming, of course, but as soon as I was imprisoned the fear of being kicked quenched all noise. I hardly dared breathe. My only hope was in motionless silence. Imagine the agony I endured! I did not steal any more of his flowers. He was a good hard judge of boy nature.

I was in Peter's hands some time before this, when I was about two and a half years old. The servant girl bathed us small folk before putting us to bed. The smarting soapy scrubbings of the Saturday nights in preparation for the Sabbath were particularly severe, and we all dreaded them. My sister Sarah, the next older than me, wanted the long-legged stool I was sitting on awaiting my turn, so she just tipped me off. My chin struck on the edge of the bath-tub, and, as I was tallying at the time, my tongue happened to be in the way of my teeth when they were closed by the blow, and a deep gash was cut on the side of it, which bled profusely. Mother came running at the noise I made, wrapped me up, put me in the servant girl's arms and told her to run with me through the garden and out by a back way to Peter Lawson to have something done to stop the bleeding. He simply rubbed a wad of cotton into my mouth after soaking it in some brown astringent stuff, and told me to be sure to keep my mouth shut and all would soon be well. Mother put me to bed, calmed my fears, and told me to lie still and sleep like a gude bairn. But just as I was dropping of to sleep I swallowed the bulky wad of medicated cotton and with it, as I imagined, my tongue also. My scream over so great a loss brought Mother, and when she anxiously took me in her arms and inquired what was the matter, I told her that I had swallowed my tongue. She only laughed at me, much to my astonishment, when I expected that she would bewail the awful loss her boy had sustained. My sisters, who were older than I, oftentimes said when I happened to be talking too much, 'It's a pity you hadn't swallowed at least half of that long tongue of yours when you were little.'

It appears natural for children to be fond of water, although the Scotch method of making every duty dismal contrived to make necessary bathing for health terrible to us. I well remember among the awful experiences of childhood being taken by the servant to the seashore when I was between two and three years old, stripped at the side of a deep pool in the rocks, plunged into it among crawling crawfish and slippery wriggling snake-like eels, and drawn up gasping and shrieking only to be plunged down again and again. As the time approached for this terrible bathing, I used to hide in the darkest corners of the house, and oftentimes a long search was required to find me. But after we were a few years older, we enjoyed bathing with other boys as we wandered along the shore, careful, however, not to get into a pool that had an invisible boy-devouring monster at the bottom of it. Such pools, miniature maelstroms, were called 'sookin-in-goats' and were well known to most of us. Nevertheless we never ventured into any pool on strange parts of the coast before we had thrust a stick into it. If the stick were not pulled out of our hands, we boldly entered and enjoyed plashing and ducking long ere we had learned to swim.

One of our best playgrounds was the famous old Dunbar Castle, to which King Edward fled after his defeat at Bannockburn. It was built more than a thousand years ago, and though we knew little of its history, we had heard many mysterious stories of the battles fought about its walls, and firmly believed that every bone we found in the ruins belonged to an ancient warrior. We tried to see who could climb highest on the crumbling peaks and crags, and took chances that no cautious mountaineer would try. That I did not fall and finish my rock-scrambling in those adventurous boyhood days seems now a reasonable wonder.

Among our best games were running, jumping, wrestling, and scrambling. I was so proud of my skill as a climber that when I first heard of hell from a servant girl who loved to tell its horrors and warn us that if we did anything wrong we would be cast into it, I always insisted that I could climb out of it. I imagined it was only a sooty pit with stone walls like those of the castle, and I felt sure there must be chinks and cracks in the masonry for fingers and toes. Anyhow the terrors of the horrible place seldom lasted long beyond the telling; for natural faith casts out fear.

Most of the Scotch children believe in ghosts, and some under peculiar conditions continue to believe in them all through life. Grave ghosts are deemed particularly dangerous, and many of the most credulous will go far out of their way to avoid passing through or near a graveyard in the dark. After being instructed by the servants in the nature, looks, and habits of the various black and white ghosts, boowuzzies, and witches we often speculated as to whether they could run fast, and tried to believe that we had a good chance to get away from most of them. To improve our speed and wind, we often took long runs into the country. Tam o'Shanter's mare outran a lot of witches – at least until she reached a place of safety beyond the keystone of the bridge – and we thought perhaps we also might be able to out-run them.

Our house formerly belonged to a physician, and a servant girl told us that the ghost of the dead doctor haunted one of the unoccupied rooms in the second story that was kept dark on account of a heavy window-tax. Our bedroom was adjacent to the ghost room, which had in it a lot of chemical apparatus – glass tubing, glass and brass retorts, test-tubes, flasks, etc – and we thought that those strange articles were still used by the old dead doctor in compounding physic. In the long summer days David and I were put to bed several hours before sunset. Mother tucked us in carefully, drew the curtains of the big old-fashioned bed, and told us to lie still and sleep like gude bairns; but we were usually out of bed, playing games of daring called 'scootchers,' about as soon as our loving mother reached the foot of the stairs, for we couldn't lie still, however hard we might try. Going into the ghost room was regarded as a very great scootcher. After venturing in a few steps and rushing back in terror, I used to dare David to go as far without getting caught.

The roof of our house, as well as the crags and walls of the old castle, offered fine mountaineering exercise. Our bedroom was lighted by a dormer window. One night I opened it in search of good scootchers and hung myself out over the slates, holding on to the sill, while the wind was making a balloon of my nightgown. I then dared David to try the adventure, and he did. Then I went out again and hung by one hand, and David did the same. Then I hung by one finger, being careful not to slip, and he did that too. Then I stood on the sill and examined the edge of the left wall of the window, crept up the slates along its side by slight finger-holds, got astride of the roof, sat there a few minutes looking at the scenery over the garden wall while the wind was howling and threatening to blow me off, then managed to slip down, catch hold of the sill, and get safely back into the room. But before attempting this scootcher, recognizing its dangerous character, with commendable caution I warned David that in case I should happen to slip I would grip the rain-trough when I was going over the eaves and hang on, and that he must then run fast downstairs and tell Father to get a ladder for me, and tell him to be quick because I would soon be tired hanging dangling in the wind by my hands. After my return from this capital scootcher, David, not to be out-done, crawled up to the top of the window-roof, and got bravely astride of it; but in trying to return he lost courage and began to greet (to cry), 'I canna get doon. Oh, I canna get doon.' I leaned out of the window and shouted encouragingly, 'Dinna greet, Davie, dinna greet, I'll help ye doon. If you greet, fayther will hear, and gee us baith an awfu' skelping.' Then, standing on the sill and holding on by one hand to the window-casing, I directed him to slip his feet down within reach, and, after securing a good hold, I jumped inside and dragged him in by his heels. This finished scootcher-scrambling for the night and frightened us into bed.

In the short winter days, when it was dark even at our early bedtime, we usually spent the hours before going to sleep playing voyages around the world under the bed-clothing. After Mother had carefully covered us, bade us goodnight and gone downstairs, we set out on our travels. Burrowing like moles, we visited France, India, America, Australia, New Zealand, and all the places we had ever heard of; our travels never ending until we fell asleep. When Mother came to take a last look at us, before she went to bed, to see that we were covered, we were oftentimes covered so well that she had difficulty in finding us, for we were hidden in all sorts of positions where sleep happened to overtake us, but in the morning we always found ourselves in good order, lying straight like gude bairns, as she said.

Some fifty years later, when I visited Scotland, I got one of my Dunbar schoolmates to introduce me to the owners of our old home, from whom I obtained permission to go up-stairs to examine our bedroom window and judge what sort of adventure getting on its roof must have been, and with all my after experience in mountaineering, I found that what I had done in daring boyhood was now beyond my skill.

Boys are often at once cruel and merciful, thoughtlessly hard-hearted and tender-hearted, sympathetic, pitiful, and kind in ever-changing contrasts. Love of neighbors, human or animal, grows up amid savage traits, coarse and fine. When Father made out to get us securely locked up in the back yard to prevent our shore and field wanderings, we had to play away the comparatively dull time as best we could. One of our amusements was hunting cats without seriously hurting them.

These sagacious animals knew, however that, though not very dangerous, boys were not to be trusted. One time in particular I remember, when we began throwing stones at an experienced old Tom, not wishing to hurt him much, though he was a tempting mark. He soon saw what we were up to, fled to the stable, and climbed to the top of the hay manger. He was still within range, however, and we kept the stones flying faster and faster, but he just blinked and played possum without wincing either at our best shots or at the noise we made. I happened to strike him pretty hard with a good-sized pebble, but he still blinked and sat still as if without feeling. 'He must be mortally wounded,' I said, 'and now we must kill him to put him out of pain,' the savage in us rapes idly growing with indulgence. All took heartily to this sort of cat mercy and began throwing the heaviest stones we could manage, but that old fellow knew what characters we were, and just as we imagined him mercifully dead he evidently thought the play was becoming too serious and that it was time to retreat; for suddenly with a wild whirr and gurr of energy he launched himself over our heads, rushed across the yard in a blur of speed, climbed to the roof of another building and over the garden wall, out of pain and bad company, with all his lives wide awake and in good working order.

After we had thus learned that Tom had at least nine lives, we tried to verify the common saying that no matter how far cats fell they always landed on their feet unhurt. We caught one in our back yard, not Tom but a smaller one of manageable size, and somehow got him smuggled up to the top story of the house. I don't know how in the world we managed to let go of him, for as soon as we opened the window and held him over the sill he knew his danger and made violent efforts to scratch and bite his way back into the room; but we determined to carry the thing through, and at last managed to drop him. I can remember to this day how the poor creature in danger of his life strained and balanced as he was falling and managed to alight on his feet. This was a cruel thing for even wild boys to do, and we never tried the experiment again, for we sincerely pitied the poor fellow when we saw him creeping slowly away, stunned and frightened, with it a swollen black and blue chin.

Again – showing the natural savagery of boys – we delighted in dog-fights, and even in the horrid red work of slaughter-houses, often running long distances and climbing over walls and roofs to see a pig killed, as soon as we heard the desperately earnest squealing. And if the butcher was good-natured, we begged him to let us get a near view of the mysterious insides and to give us a bladder to blow up for a foot-ball.

But here is an illustration of the better side of boy nature. In our back yard there were three elm trees and in the one nearest the house a pair of robin-redbreasts had their nest. When the young were almost able to fly, a troop of the celebrated 'Scottish Grays' visited Dunbar, and three or four of the fine horses were lodged in our stable. When the soldiers were polishing their swords and helmets, they happened to notice the nest, and just as they were leaving, one of them climbed the tree and robbed it. With sore sympathy we watched the young birds as the hard-hearted robber pushed them one by one beneath his jacket – all but two that jumped out of the nest and tried to fly, but they were easily caught as they fluttered on the ground, and were hidden away with the rest. The distress of the bereaved parents, as they hovered and screamed over the frightened crying children they so long had loved and sheltered and fed, was pitiful to see; but the shining soldier rode grandly away on his big gray horse, caring only for the few pennies the young songbirds would bring and the beer they would buy, while we all, sisters and brothers, were crying and sobbing. I remember, as if it happened this day, how my heart fairly ached and choked me. Mother put us to bed and tried to comfort us, telling us that the little birds would be well fed and grow big, and soon learn to sing in pretty cages; but again and again we rehearsed the sad story of the poor bereaved birds and their frightened children, and could not be comforted. Father came into the room when we were half asleep and still sobbing, and I heard Mother telling him that 'a' the bairns' hearts were broken over the robbing of the nest in the elm.'

After attaining the manly, belligerent age of five or fix years, very few of my schooldays passed without a fist fight, and half a dozen was no uncommon number. When any classmate of our own age questioned our rank and standing as fighters, we always made haste to settle the matter at a quiet place on the Davel Brae. To be a 'gude fechter' was our highest ambition, our dearest aim in life in or out of school. To be a good scholar was a secondary consideration, though we tried hard to hold high places in our classes and gloried in being Dux. We fairly reveled in the battle stories of glorious William Wallace and Robert the Bruce, with which every breath of Scotch air is saturated, and of course we were all going to be soldiers. On the Davel Brae battleground we often managed to bring on something like real war, greatly more exciting than personal combat. Choosing leaders, we divided into two armies. In winter damp snow furnished plenty of ammunition to make the thing serious, and in summer sand and grass sods. Cheering and shouting some battle-cry such as 'Bannockburn! Bannockburn! Scotland forever! The Last War in India!' we were led bravely on. For heavy battery work we stuffed our Scotch blue bonnets with snow and sand, sometimes mixed with gravel, and fired them at each other as cannon-balls.

Of course we always looked eagerly forward to vacation days and thought them slow in coming. Old Mungo Siddons gave us a lot of gooseberries or currants and wished us a happy time. Some sort of special closing-exercises – diggings, recitations, etc – celebrated the great day, but I remember only the berries, freedom from school work, and opportunities for runaway rambles in the fields and along the wave-beaten seashore.

An exciting time came when at the age of seven or eight years I left the auld Davel Brae school for the grammar school. Of course I had a terrible lot of fighting to do, because a new scholar had to meet every one of his age who dared to challenge him, this being the common introduction to a new school. It was very strenuous for the first month or so, establishing my fighting rank, taking up new studies, especially Latin and French, getting acquainted with new classmates and the master and his rules. In the first few Latin and French lessons the new teacher, Mr Lyon, blandly smiled at our comical blunders, but pedagogical weather of the severest kind quickly set in, when for every mistake, everything short of perfection, the taws was promptly applied. We had to get three lessons every day in Latin, three in French, and as many in English, besides spelling, history, arithmetic, and geography. Word lessons in particular, the wouldst-couldst-shouldst-have-loved kind, were kept up, with much warlike thrashing, until I had committed the whole of the French, Latin, and English grammars to memory, and in connection with reading-lessons we were called on to recite parts of them with the rules over and over again, as if all the regular and irregular incomprehensible verb stuff was poetry. In addition to all this, Father made me learn so many Bible verses every day that by the time I was eleven years of age I had about three fourths of the Old Testament and all of the New by heart and by sore flesh. I could recite the New Testament from the beginning of Matthew to the end of Revelation without a single stop. The dangers of cramming and of making scholars study at home instead of letting their little brains rest were never heard of in those days. We carried our school-books home in a strap every night and committed to memory our next day's lessons before we went to bed, and to do that we had to bend our attention as closely on our tasks as lawyers on great million-dollar cases. I can't conceive of anything that would now enable me to concentrate my attention more fully than when I was a mere stripling boy, and it was all done by whipping – thrashing in general. Old-fashioned Scotch teachers spent no time in seeking short roads to knowledge, or in trying any of the new-fangled psychological methods so much in vogue nowadays. There was nothing said about making the seats easy or the lessons easy. We were simply driven pointblank against our books like soldiers against the enemy, and sternly ordered, 'Up and at 'em. Commit your lessons to memory!' If we failed in any part, however slight, we were whipped; for the grand, simple, all-sufficing Scotch discovery had been made that there was a close connection between the skin and the memory, and that irritating the skin excited the memory to any required degree.

Fighting was carried on still more vigorously in the high school than in the common school. Whenever anyone was challenged, either the challenge was allowed or it was decided by a battle on the seashore, where with stubborn enthusiasm we battered each other as if we had not been sufficiently battered by the teacher. When we were so fortunate as to finish a fight without getting a black eye, we usually escaped a thrashing at home and another next morning at school, for other traces of the fray could be easily washed off at a well on the church brae, or concealed, or passed as results of play-ground accidents; but a black eye could never be explained away from downright fighting. A good double thrashing was the inevitable penalty, but without avail; fighting went on without the slightest abatement, like natural storms; for no punishment less than death could quench the ancient inherited belligerence burning in our pagan blood. Nor could we be made to believe it was fair that Father and teacher should thrash us so industriously for our good, while begrudging us the pleasure of thrashing each other for our good. All these various thrashings, however, were admirably influential in developing not only memory but fortitude as well. For if we did not endure our school punishments and fighting pains without flinching and making faces, we were mocked on the playground, and public opinion on a Scotch playground was a powerful agent in controlling behavior; therefore we at length managed to keep our features in smooth repose while enduring pain that would try anybody but an American Indian. Far from feeling that we were called on to endure too much pain, one of our playground games was thrashing each other with whips about two feet long made from the tough, wiry stems of a species of polygonum fastened together in a stiff, firm braid. One of us handing two of these whips to a companion to take his choice, we stood up close together and thrashed each other on the legs until one succumbed to the intolerable pain and thus lost the game. Nearly all of our playground games were strenuous – shin-battering shinny, wrestling, prisoners' base, and dogs and hares – all augmenting in no slight degree our lessons in fortitude. Moreover, we regarded our punishments and pains of every sort as training for war, since we were all going to be soldiers. Besides single combats we sometimes assembled on Saturdays to meet the scholars of another school and very little was required for the growth of strained relations, and war. The immediate cause might be nothing more than a saucy stare. Perhaps the scholar stared at would insolently inquire, 'What are ye glowerin' at, Bob?' Bob would reply, 'I'll look where I hae a mind and hinder me if ye daur.' 'Weel, Bob,' the outraged stared-at scholar would reply, 'I'll soon let ye see whether I daur or no,' and give Bob a blow on the face. This opened the battle, and every good scholar belonging to either school was drawn into it. After both sides were sore and weary, a strong lunged warrior would be heard above the din of battle shouting, 'I'll tell ye what we'll dae wi' ye. If ye'll let us alone we'll let ye alane!' and the school war ended as most wars between nations do; and some of them begin in much the same way.

Notwithstanding the great number of harshly enforced rules, not very good order was kept in school in my time. There were two schools within a few roods of each other, one for mathematics, navigation, etc., the other, called the grammar school, that I attended. The masters lived in a big freestone house within eight or ten yards of the schools, so that they could easily step out for anything they wanted or send one of the scholars. The moment our master disappeared, perhaps for a book or a drink, every scholar left his seat and his lessons, jumped on top of the benches and desks or crawled beneath them, tugging, rolling, wrestling, accomplishing in a minute a depth of disorder and din unbelievable save by a Scottish scholar. We even carried on war, class against class, in those wild, precious minutes. A watcher gave the alarm when the master opened his house-door to return, and it was a great feat to get into our places before he entered, adorned in awful majestic authority shouting 'Silence!' and striking resounding blows with his cane on a desk or on some unfortunate scholar's back.

Forty-seven years after leaving this fighting school, I returned on a visit to Scotland, and a cousin in Dunbar introduced me to a minister who was acquainted with the history of the school, and obtained for me an invitation to dine with the new master. Of course I gladly accepted, for I wanted to see the old place of fun and pain, and the battleground on the sands. Mr Lyon, our able teacher and thrasher, I learned, had held his place as master of the school for twenty or thirty years after I left it, and had recently died in London, after preparing many young men for the English Universities. At the dinner-table, while I was recalling the amusements and fights of my old school-days, the minister remarked to the new master, 'Now, don't you wish that you had been teacher in those days, and gained the honor of walloping John Muir?' This pleasure so merrily suggested showed that the minister also had been a fighter in his youth. The old freestone school building was still perfectly sound, but the carved, ink-stained desks were almost whittled away.

The highest part of our playground back of the school commanded a view of the sea, and we loved to watch the passing ships and, judging by their rigging, make guesses as to the ports they had sailed from, those to which they were bound, what they were loaded with, their tonnage, etc. In stormy weather they were all smothered in clouds and spray, and showers of salt scud torn from the tops of the waves came flying over the playground wall. In those tremendous storms many a brave ship foundered or was tossed and smashed on the rocky shore. When a wreck occurred within a mile or two of the town, we often managed by running fast to reach it and pick up some of the spoils. In particular I remember visiting the battered fragments of an unfortunate brig or schooner that had been loaded with apples, and finding fine unpitiful sport in rushing into the spent waves and picking up the red-cheeked fruit from the frothy, seething foam.

All our school-books were extravagantly illustrated with drawings of every kind of sailing-vessel, and every boy owned some sort of craft whittled from a block of wood and trimmed with infinite pains – sloops, schooners, brigs, and full-rigged ships, with their sails and string ropes properly adjusted and named for us by some old sailor. These precious toy craft with lead keels we learned to sail on a pond near the town. With the sails set at the proper angle to the wind, they made fast straight voyages across the pond to boys on the other side, who readjusted the sails and started them back on the return voyages. Oftentimes fleets of half a dozen or more were started together in exciting races.

Our most exciting sport, however, was playing with gunpowder. We made guns out of gas-pipe, mounted them on sticks of any shape, clubbed our pennies together for powder, gleaned pieces of lead here and there and cut them into slugs, and, while one aimed, another applied a match to the touch-hole. With these awful weapons we wandered along the beach and fired at the gulls and solan-geese as they passed us. Fortunately we never hurt any of them that we knew of. We also dug holes in the ground, put in a handful or two of powder, tamped it well around a fuse made of a wheat-stalk, and, reaching cautiously forward, touched a match to the straw. This we called making earthquakes. Oftentimes we went home with singed hair and faces well peppered with powder-grains that could not be washed out. Then, of course, came a correspondingly severe punishment from both Father and teacher.

Another favorite sport was climbing trees and scaling garden-walls. Boys eight or ten years of age could get over almost any wall by standing on each other's shoulders, thus making living ladders. To make walls secure against marauders, many of them were finished on top with broken bottles imbedded in lime, leaving the cutting edges sticking up; but with bunches of grass and weeds we could sit or stand in comfort on top of the jaggedest of them.

Like squirrels that begin to eat nuts before they are ripe, we began to eat apples about as soon as they were formed, causing, of course, desperate gastric disturbances to be cured by castor oil. Serious were the risks we ran in climbing and squeezing through hedges, and, of course, among the country folk we were far from welcome. Farmers passing us on the roads often shouted by way of greeting: 'Oh, you vagabonds! Back to the toon wi' ye. Gang back where ye belang. You're up to mischief Ise warrant. I can see it. The gamekeeper'll catch ye, and maist like ye'll a' be hanged some day.'

Breakfast in those auld-lang-syne days was simple oatmeal porridge, usually with a little milk or treacle, served in wooden dishes called 'luggies,' formed of staves hooped together like miniature tubs about four or five inches in diameter. One of the staves, the lug or ear, a few inches longer than the others, served as a handle, while the number of luggies ranged in a row on a dresser indicated the size of the family. We never dreamed of anything to come after the porridge, or of asking for more. Our portions were consumed in about a couple of minutes; then off to school. At noon we came racing home ravenously hungry. The midday meal, called dinner, was usually vegetable broth, a small piece of boiled mutton, and barley-meal scone. None of us liked the barley scone bread, therefore we got all we wanted of it, and in desperation had to eat it, for we were always hungry, about as hungry after as before meals. The evening meal was called 'tea' and was served on our return from school. It consisted, as far as we children were concerned, of half a slice of white bread without butter, barley scone, and warm water with a little milk and sugar in it, a beverage called 'content,' which warmed but neither cheered nor inebriated. Immediately after tea we ran across the street with our books to Grandfather Gilrye, who took pleasure in seeing us and hearing us recite our next day's lessons. Then back home to supper, usually a boiled potato and piece of barley scone. Then family worship, and to bed.

Our amusements on Saturday afternoons and vacations depended mostly on getting away from home into the country, especially in the spring when the birds were calling loudest. Father sternly forbade David and me from playing truant in the fields with plundering wanderers like ourselves, fearing we might go on from bad to worse, get hurt in climbing over walls, caught by gamekeepers, or lost by falling over a cliff into the sea. 'Play as much as you like in the back yard and garden,' he said, 'and mind what you'll get when you forget and disobey.' Thus he warned us with an awfully stern countenance, looking very hard-hearted, while naturally his heart was far from hard, though he devoutly believed in eternal punishment for bad boys both here and hereafter. Nevertheless, like devout martyrs of wildness, we stole away to the seashore or the green, sunny fields with almost religious regularity, taking advantage of opportunities when Father was very busy, to join our companions, oftenest to hear the birds sing and hunt their nests, glorying in the number we had discovered and called our own. A sample of our nest chatter was something like this: Willie Chisholm would proudly exclaim – 'I ken [know] seventeen nests, and you, Johnnie, ken only fifteen.'

'But I wouldna gie my fifteen for your seventeen, for five of mine are larks and mavises. You ken only three o' the best singers.'

'Yes, Johnnie, but I ken six goldies and you ken only one. Maist of yours are only sparrows and linties and robin-redbreasts.'

Then perhaps Bob Richardson would loudly declare that he 'kenned mair nests than onybody, for he kenned twenty-three, with about fifty eggs in them and mair than fifty young birds – maybe a hundred. Some of them naething but raw gorblings but lots of them as big as their mithers and ready to flee. And aboot fifty craw's nests and three fox dens.'

'Oh, yes, Bob, but that's no fair, for naebody counts craw's nests and fox holes, and then you live in the country at Bellehaven where ye have the best chance.'

'Yes, but I ken a lot of bumbee's nests, baith the red-legged and the yellow-legged kind.'

'Oh, wha cares for bumbee's nests!'

'Weel, but here's something! Ma father let me gang to a fox hunt, and man, it was grand to see the hounds and the lang-legged horses lowpin the dykes and burns and hedges!'

The nests, I fear, with the beautiful eggs and young birds, were prized quite as highly as the songs of the glad parents, but no Scotch boy that I know of ever failed to listen with enthusiasm to the songs of the skylarks. Oftentimes on a broad meadow near Dunbar we stood for hours enjoying their marvelous singing and soaring. From the grass where the nest was hidden the male would suddenly rise, as straight as if shot up, to a height of perhaps thirty or forty feet, and, sustaining himself with rapid wing-beats, pour down the most delicious melody, sweet and cleat and strong, overflowing all bounds, then suddenly he would soar higher again and again, ever higher and higher, soaring and singing until lost to sight even on perfectly clear days, and oftentimes in cloudy weather 'far in the downy cloud,' as the poet says.

To test our eyes we often watched a lark until he seemed a faint speck in the sky and finally passed beyond the keenest-sighted of us all. 'I see him yet!' we would cry, 'I see him yet!' 'I see him yet!' 'I see him yet!' as he soared. And finally only one of us would be left to claim that he still saw him. At last he, too, would have to admit that the singer had soared beyond his sight, and still the music came pouring down to us in glorious profusion, from a height far above our vision, requiring marvelous power of wing and marvelous power of voice, for that rich, delicious, soft, and yet clear music was distinctly heard long after the bird was out of sight. Then, suddenly ceasing, the glorious singer would appear, falling like a bolt straight down to his nest, where his mate was sitting on the eggs.

It was far too common a practice among us to carry off a young lark just before it could fly, place it in a cage, and fondly, laboriously feed it. Sometimes we succeeded in keeping one alive for a year or two, and when awakened by the spring weather it was pitiful to see the quivering imprisoned soarer of the heavens rapidly beating its wings and singing as though it were flying and hovering in the air like its parents. To keep it in health we were taught that we must supply it with a sod of grass the size of the bottom of the cage, to make the poor bird feel as though it were at home on its native meadow – a meadow perhaps a foot or at most two feet square. Again and again it would try to hover over that miniature meadow from its miniature sky just underneath the top of the cage. At last, conscience-stricken, we carried the beloved prisoner to the meadow west of Dunbar where it was born, and, blessing its sweet heart, bravely set it free, and our exceeding great reward was to see it fly and sing in the sky.

In the winter, when there was but little doing in the fields, we organized running-matches. A dozen or so of us would start out on races that were simply tests of endurance, running on and on along a public road over the breezy hills like hounds, without stopping or getting tired. The only serious trouble we ever felt in these long races was an occasional stitch in our sides. One of the boys started the story that sucking raw eggs was a sure cure for the stitches. We had hens in our back yard, and on the next Saturday we managed to swallow a couple of eggs apiece, a disgusting job, but we would do almost anything to mend our speed, and as soon as we could get away after taking the cure we set out on a ten or twenty mile run to prove its worth. We thought nothing of running right ahead ten or a dozen miles before turning back; for we knew nothing about taking time by the suns and none of us had a watch in those days. Indeed, we never cared about time until it began to get dark. Then we thought of home and the thrashing that awaited us. Late or early, the thrashing was sure, unless Father happened to be away. If he was expected to return soon, Mother made haste to get us to bed before his arrival. We escaped the thrashing next morning, for Father never felt like thrashing us in cold blood on the calm holy Sabbath. But no punishment, however sure and severe, was of any avail against the attraction of the fields and woods. It had other uses, developing memory, etc., but in keeping us at home it was of no use at all. Wildness was ever sounding in our ears, and Nature saw to it that besides school lessons and church lessons some of her own lessons should be learned, perhaps with a view to the time when we should be called to wander in wildness to our heart's content. Oh, the blessed enchantment of those Saturday runaways in the prime of the spring! How our young wondering eyes reveled in the sunny, breezy glory of the hills and the sky, every particle of us thrilling and tingling with the bees and glad birds and glad streams! Kings may be blessed; we were glorious, we were free – school cares and scoldings, heart thrashings and flesh thrashings alike, were forgotten in the fullness of Nature's glad wildness. These were my first excursions – the beginnings of lifelong wanderings.

Chapter 2

A NEW WORLD

Our grammar-school reader, called, I think, 'Maccoulough's Course of Reading', contained a few natural-history sketches that excited me very much and left a deep impression, especially a fine description of the fish hawk and the bald eagle by the Scotch ornithologist Wilson, who had the good fortune to wander for years in the American woods while the country was yet mostly wild. I read his description over and over again, till I got the vivid picture he drew by heart – the long-winged hawk circling over the heaving waves, every motion watched by the eagle perched on the top of a crag or dead tree; the fish hawk poising for a moment to take aim at a fish and plunging under the water; the eagle with kindling eye spreading his wings ready for instant flight in case the attack should prove successful; the hawk emerging with a struggling fish in his talons, and proud flight; the eagle launching himself in pursuit; the wonderful wing-work in the sky, the fish hawk, though encumbered with his prey, circling higher, higher, striving hard to keep above the robber eagle; the eagle at length soaring above him, compel him with a cry of despair to drop his hard-won prey; then the eagle steadying himself for a moment to take aim, descending swift as a lightning-bolt, and dog the falling fish before it reached the sea.

Not less exciting and memorable was Audubon's wonderful story of the passenger pigeon, a beautiful bird flying in vast flocks that darkened the sky like clouds, countless millions ambling to rest and sleep and rear their young in certain forests, miles in length and breadth, fifty or a hundred nests on a single tree; the overloaded branches bending low and often breaking; the farmers gathering from far and near, beating down countless thousands of the young and old birds from their nests and roosts with long poles at Bight, and in the morning driving their bands of hogs, some of them brought from farms a hundred miles distant, to fatten on the dead and wounded covering the ground.

In another of our reading-lessons some of the American forests were described. The most interesting of the trees to us boys was the sugar maple, and soon after we had learned this sweet story we heard everybody talking about the discovery of gold in the same wonder-filled country.

One night, when David and I were at Grandfather's fireside solemnly learning our lessons as usual, my father came in with news, the most wonderful, most glorious, that wild boys ever heard. 'Bairns,' he said, 'you needna learn your lessons the nicht, for we're gan to America the morn!' No more grammar, but boundless woods full of mysterious good things; trees full of sugar, growing in ground full of gold; hawks, eagles, pigeons, filling the sky; millions of birds' nests, and no game-keepers to stop us in all the wild, happy land. We were utterly, blindly glorious. After Father left the room, Grandfather gave David and me a gold coin apiece for a keepsake, and looked very serious, for he was about to be deserted in his lonely old age. And when we in fullness of young joy spoke of what we were going to do, of the wonderful birds and their nests that we should find, the sugar and gold, etc., and promised to send him a big box full of that tree sugar packed in gold from the glorious paradise over the sea, poor lonely Grandfather, about to be forsaken, looked with downcast eyes on the floor and said in a low, trembling, troubled voice, 'Ah, poor laddies, poor laddies, you'll find something else ower the sea forbye gold and sugar, birds' nests and freedom fra lessons and schools. You'll find plenty hard, hard work.' And so we did. But nothing he could say could cloud our joy or abate the fire of youthful, hopeful, fearless adventure. Nor could we in the midst of such measureless excitement see or feel the shadows and sorrows of his darkening old age. To my school-mates, met that night on the street, I shouted the glorious news, 'I'm gan to Amaraka the morn!' None could believe it. I said, 'Weel, just you see if I am at the skule the morn!'

Next morning we went by rail to Glasgow and thence joyfully sailed away from beloved Scotland, flying to our fortunes on the wings of the winds, carefree as thistle seeds. We could not then know what we were leaving, what we were to encounter in the New World, nor what our gains were likely to be. We were too young and full of hope for fear or regret, but not too young to look forward with eager enthusiasm to the wonderful schoolless, bookless American wilderness. Even the natural heart-pain of parting from Grandfather and Grandmother Gilrye, who loved us so well, and from Mother and sisters and brother, was quickly quenched in young joy. Father took with him only my sister Sarah (thirteen years of age), myself (eleven), and brother David (nine), leaving my eldest sister, Margaret, and the three youngest of the family, Daniel, Mary, and Anna, with Mother, to join us after a farm had been found in the wilderness and a comfortable house made to receive them.

In crossing the Atlantic before the days of steamships, or even the American clippers, the voyages made in old-fashioned sailing-vessels were very long. Ours was six weeks and three days. But because we had no lessons to get, that long voyage had not a dull moment for us boys. Father and sister Sarah, with most of the old folk, stayed below in rough weather, groaning in the miseries of seasickness, many of the passengers wishing they had never ventured in 'the auld rockin' creel,' as they called our bluff-bowed, wave-beating ship, and, when the weather was moderately calm, singing songs in the evenings – 'The Youthful Sailor Frank and Bold,' 'Oh, why left I my hame, why did I cross the deep,' etc. But no matter how much the old tub tossed about and battered the waves, we were on deck every day, not in the least seasick, watching the sailors at their rope-hauling and climbing work; joining in their songs, learning the names of the ropes and sails, and helping them as far as they would let us; playing games with other boys in calm weather when the deck was dry, and in stormy weather rejoicing in sympathy with the big curly-topped waves.

The captain occasionally called David and me into his cabin and asked us about our schools, handed us books to read, and seemed surprised to find that Scotch boys could read and pronounce English with perfect accent and knew so much Latin and French. In Scotch schools only pure English was taught, although not a word of English was spoken out of school. All through life, however well-educated, the Scotch spoke Scotch among their own folk, except at times when unduly excited on the only two subjects on which Scotchmen get much excited, namely, religion and politics. So long as the controversy went on with fairly level temper, only gude braid Scots was used, but if one became angry, as was likely to happen, then he immediately began speaking severely correct English, while his antagonist, drawing himself up, would say: 'Weel, there's na use pursuing this subject ony further, for I see ye hae gotten to your English.'

As we neared the shore of the great new land, with what eager wonder we watched the whales and dolphins and porpoises and seabirds, and made the good-natured sailors teach us their names and tell us stories about them!'

There were quite a large number of emigrants aboard, many of them newly married couples, and the advantages of the different parts of the New World they expected to settle in were often discussed. My father started with the intention of going to the backwoods of Upper Canada. Before the end of the voyage, however, he was persuaded that the States offered superior advantages, especially Wisconsin and Michigan, where the land was said to be as good as in Canada and far more easily brought under cultivation; for in Canada the woods were so close and heavy that a man might wear out his life in getting a few acres cleared of trees and stumps. So he changed his mind and concluded to go to one of the Western States.

On our wavering westward way a grain-dealer in Buffalo told Father that most of the wheat he handled came from

Wisconsin; and this influential information finally determined my father's choice. At Milwaukee a farmer who had come in from the country near Fort Winnebago with a load of wheat agreed to haul us and our formidable load of stuff to a little town called Kingston for thirty dollars. On that hundred-mile journey, just after the spring thaw, the roads over the prairies were heavy and miry, causing no end of lamentation, for we often got stuck in the mud, and the poor farmer sadly declared that never, never again would he be tempted to try to haul such a cruel, heart-breaking, wagon-breaking, horse-killing load, no, not for a hundred dollars. In leaving Scotland, Father, like many other home-seekers, burdened himself with far too much luggages as if all America were still a wilderness in which little or nothing could be bought. One of his big iron-bound boxes must have weighed about four hundred pounds, for it contained an old-fashioned beam-scales with a complete set of cast-iron counterweights, two of them fifty-six pounds each, a twenty-eight, and so on down to a single pound. Also a lot of iron wedges, carpenter's tools, and so forth, and at Buffalo as if on the very edge of the wilderness, he gladly added to his burden a big cast-iron stove with pots and pans, provisions enough for a long siege, and a scythe and cumbersome cradle for cutting wheat, all of which he succeeded in landing in the primeval Wisconsin woods.

A land-agent at Kingston gave Father a note to a farmer by the name of Alexander Gray, who lived on the border of the settled part of the country, knew the section-lines, and would probably help him to find a good place for a farm. So Father went away to spy out the land, and in the meantime left us children in Kingston in a rented room. It took us less than an hour to get acquainted with some of the boys in the village; we challenged them to wrestle, run races, climb trees, etc., and in a day or two we felt at home, carefree and happy, notwithstanding our family was so widely divided. When Father returned he told us that he had found fine land for a farm in sunny open woods on the side of a lake, and that a team of three yoke of oxen with a big wagon was coming to haul us to Mr Gray's place.

We enjoyed the strange ten-mile ride through the woods very much, wondering how the great oxen could be so strong and wise and tame as to pull so heavy a load with no other harness than a chain and a crooked piece of wood on their necks, and how they could sway so obediently to right and left past road-side trees and stumps when the driver said *haw* and *gee*. At Mr Gray's house, Father again left us for a few days to build a shanty on the quarter-section he had selected four or five miles to the westward. In the meanwhile we enjoyed our freedom as usual, wandering in the fields and meadows, looking at the trees and flowers, snakes and birds and squirrels. With the help of the nearest neighbors the little shanty was built in less than a day after the rough bur-oak logs for the walls and the white-oak boards for the floor and roof were got together.

To this charming hut, in the sunny woods, overlooking a flowery glacier meadow and a lake rimmed with white water-lilies, we were hauled by an ox-team across trackless carex swamps and low rolling hills sparely dotted with round-headed oaks. Just as we arrived at the shanty, before we had time to look at it or the scenery about it, David and I jumped down in a hurry off the load of household goods, for we had discovered a blue jay's nest, and in a minute or so we were up the tree beside it, feasting our eyes on the beautiful green eggs and beautiful birds – our first memorable discovery. The handsome birds had not seen Scotch boys before and made a desperate screaming as if we were robbers like themselves, though we left the eggs untouched, feeling that we were already beginning to get rich, and wondering how many more nests we should find in the grand sunny woods. Then we ran along the brow of the hill that the shanty stood on, and down to the meadow, searching the trees and grass tufts and bushes, and soon discovered a bluebird's and a woodpecker's nest, and began an acquaintance with the frogs and snakes and turtles in the creeks and springs.

This sudden plash into pure wildness – baptism in Nature's warm heart – how utterly happy it made us! Nature streaming into us, wooingly teaching her wonderful glowing lessons, so unlike the dismal grammar ashes and cinders so long thrashed into us. Here without knowing it we still were at school; every wild lesson a love lesson, not whipped but charmed into us. Oh, that glorious Wisconsin wilderness! Everything new and pure in the very prime of the spring when Nature's pulses were beating highest and mysteriously keeping time with our own! Young hearts, young leaves, flowers, animals, the winds and the streams and the sparkling lake, all wildly, gladly rejoicing together!

Next morning, when we climbed to the precious jay nest to take another admiring look at the eggs, we found it empty. Not a shell-fragment was left, and we wondered how in the world the birds were able to carry off their thin-shelled eggs either in their bills or in their feet without breaking them, and how they could be kept warm while a new nest was being built. Well, I am still asking these questions. When I was on the Harriman Expedition I asked Robert Ridgway, the eminent ornithologist, how these sudden flittings were accomplished, and he frankly confessed that he didn't know, but guessed that jays and many other birds carried their eggs in their mouths; and when I objected that a jay's mouth seemed too small to hold its eggs, he replied that birds' mouths were larger than the narrowness of their bills indicated. Then I asked him what he thought they did with the eggs while a new nest was being prepared. He didn't know; neither do I to this day. A specimen of the many puzzling problems presented to the naturalist.

We soon found many more nests belonging to birds that were not half so suspicious. The handsome and notorious blue jay plunders the nests of other birds and of course he could not trust us. Almost all the others – brown thrushes, bluebirds, song sparrows, kingbirds, hen-hawks, nighthawks, whip-poor-wills, woodpeckers, etc – simply tried to avoid being seen, to draw or drive us away, or paid no attention to us.

We used to wonder how the woodpeckers could bore holes so perfectly round, true mathematical circles. We ourselves could not have done it even with gouges and chisels. We loved to watch them feeding their young, and wondered how they could glean food enough for so many clamorous, hungry, unsatisfiable babies, and how they managed to give each one its share; for after the young grew strong, one would get his head out of the door-hole and try to hold possession of it to meet the food-laden parents. How hard they worked to support their families, especially the red-headed and speckledy woodpeckers and flickers; digging, hammering on scaly bark and decaying trunks and branches from dawn to dark, coming and going at intervals of a few minutes all the live-long day!

We discovered a hen-hawk's nest on the top of a tall oak thirty or forty rods from the shanty and approached it cautiously. One of the pair always kept watch, soaring in wide circles high above the tree, and when we attempted to climb it, the big dangerous-looking bird came swooping down at us and drove us away.

We greatly admired the plucky kingbird. In Scotland our great ambition was to be good fighters, and we admired this quality in the handsome little chattering flycatcher that whips all the other birds. He was particularly angry when plundering jays and hawks came near his home, and took pains to thrash them not only away from the nest-tree but out of the neighborhood. The nest was usually built on a bur oak near a meadow where insects were abundant, and where no undesirable visitor could approach without being discovered. When a hen-hawk hove in sight, the male immediately set off after him, and it was ridiculous to see that great, strong bird hurrying away as fast as his clumsy wings would carry him, as soon as he saw the little, waspish kingbird coming. But the kingbird easily overtook him, flew just a few feet above him, and with a lot of chattering, scolding notes kept diving and striking him on the back of the head until tired; then he alighted to rest on the hawk's broad shoulders, still scolding and chattering as he rode along, like an angry boy pouring out vials of wrath. Then, up and at him again with his sharp bill; and after he had thus driven and ridden his big enemy a mile or so from the nest, he went home to his mate, chuckling and bragging as if trying to tell her what a wonderful fellow he was.

This first spring, while some of the birds were still building their nests and very few young ones had yet tried to fly, Father hired a Yankee to assist in clearing eight or ten acres of the best ground for a field. We found new wonders every day and often had to call on this Yankee to solve puzzling questions. We asked him one day if there was any bird in America that the kingbird couldn't whip. What about the sandhill crane? Could he whip that long-legged, long-billed fellow?

'A crane never goes near kingbirds' nests or notices so small a bird,' he said, 'and therefore there could be no fighting between them.' So we hastily concluded that our hero could whip every bird in the country except perhaps the sandhill crane.

We never tired listening to the wonderful whip-poor-will. One came every night about dusk and sat on a log about twenty or thirty feet from our cabin door and began shouting 'Whip poor Will! Whip poor Will!' with loud emphatic earnestness. 'What's that? What's that?' we cried when this startling visitor first announced himself. 'What do you call it?'

'Why, it's telling you its name,' said the Yankee. 'Don't you hear it and what he wants you to do? He says his name is "Poor Will" and he wants you to whip him, and you may if you are able to catch him.' Poor Will seemed the most wonderful of all the strange creatures we had seen. What a wild, strong, bold voice he had, unlike any other we had ever heard on sea or land!

A near relative, the bull-bat, or nighthawk, seemed hardly less wonderful. Towards evening scattered flocks kept the sky lively as they circled around on their long wings a hundred feet or more above the ground, hunting moths and beetles, interrupting their rather slow but strong, regular wing-beats at short intervals with quick quivering strokes while uttering keen, squeaky cries something like *pfee*, *pfee*, and every now and then diving nearly to the ground with a loud ripping, bellowing sound, like bull-roaring, suggesting its name; then turning and gliding swiftly up again. These fine wild gray birds, about the size of a pigeon, lay their two eggs on bare ground without anything like a nest or even a concealing bush or grass-tuft. Nevertheless they are not easily seen, for they are colored like the ground. While sitting on their eggs, they depend so much upon not being noticed that if you are walking rapidly ahead they allow you to step within an inch or two of them without flinching. But if they see by your looks that you have discovered them, they leave their eggs or young, and, like a good many other birds, pretend that they are sorely wounded, fluttering and rolling over on the ground and gasping as if dying, to draw you away. When pursued we were surprised to find that just when we were on the point of overtaking them they were always able to flutter a few yards farther, until they had led us about a quarter of a mile from the nest; then, suddenly getting well, they quietly flew home by a roundabout way to their precious babies or eggs o'er a' the ills of life victorious, bad boys among the worst. The Yankee took particular pleasure in encouraging us to pursue them.

Everything about us was so novel and wonderful that we could hardly believe our senses except when hungry or while Father was thrashing us. When we first saw Fountain Lake Meadow, on a sultry evening, sprinkled with millions of lightning-bugs throbbing with light, the effect was so strange and beautiful that it seemed far too marvelous to be real. Looking from our shanty on the hill, I thought that the whole wonderful fairy show must be in my eyes; for only in fighting, when my eyes were struck, had I ever seen anything in the least like it. But when I asked my brother if he saw anything strange in the meadow he said, 'Yes, it's all covered with shaky fire-sparks.' Then I guessed that it might be something outside of us, and applied to our all-knowing Yankee to explain it. 'Oh, it's nothing but lightnin'-bugs,' he said, and kindly led us down the hill to the edge of the fiery meadow, caught a few of the wonderful bugs, dropped them into a cup, and carried them to the shanty, where we watched them throbbing and flashing out their mysterious light at regular intervals, as if each little passionate glow were caused by the beating of a heart. Once I saw a splendid display of glow-worm light in the foothills of the Himalayas, north of Calcutta, but glorious as it appeared in pure starry radiance, it was far less impressive than the extravagant abounding, quivering, dancing fire on our Wisconsin meadow.

Partridge drumming was another great marvel. When I first heard the low, soft, solemn sound I thought it must be made by some strange disturbance in my head or stomach, but as all seemed serene within, I asked David whether he heard anything queer. 'Yes,' he said, 'I hear something saying *boomp*, *boomp*, *boomp*, and I'm wondering at it.' Then I was half satisfied that the source of the mysterious sound must be in something outside of us, coming perhaps from the ground or from some ghost or bogie or woodland fairy. Only after long watching and listening did we at last discover it in the wings of the plump brown bird.

The love-song of the common jack snipe seemed not a whit less mysterious than partridge drumming. It was usually heard on cloudy evenings, a strange, unearthly, winnowing, spiritlike sound, yet easily heard at a distance of a third of a mile. Our sharp eyes soon detected the bird while making it, as it circled high in the air over the meadow with wonderfully strong and rapid wing-beats, suddenly descending and rising, again and again, in deep, wide loops; the tones being very low and smooth at the beginning of the descent, rapidly increasing to a curious little whirling storm-roar at the bottom, and gradually fading lower and lower until the top was reached. It was long, however, before we identified this mysterious wing-singer as the little brown jack snipe that we knew so well and had so often watched as he silently probed the mud around the edge of our meadow stream and spring-holes, and made short zigzag flights over the grass uttering only little short, crisp quacks and chucks.

The love-songs of the frogs seemed hardly less wonderful than those of the birds, their musical notes varying from the sweet, tranquil, soothing peeping and purring of the hylas to the awfully deep low-bass blunt bellowing of the bullfrogs. Some of the smaller species have wonderfully clear, sharp

voices and told us their good Bible names in musical tones
about as plainly as the whip-poor-will. *Isaac, Isaac; Yacob,
Yacob; Israel, Israel;* shouted in sharp, ringing, far-reaching
tones, as if they had all been to school and severely drilled in
elocution. In the still, warm evenings big bunchy bullfrogs
bellowed, *Drunk! Drunk! Drunk! Jug o' rum! Jug o' rum!* and
early in the spring, counts less thousands of the commonest
species, up to the throat in cold water, sang in concert, making
a mass of music, such as it was, loud enough to be heard at a
distance of more than half a mile.

Far, far apart from this loud marsh music is that of the many
species of hyla, a sort of soothing immortal melody filling the
air like light.

We reveled in the glory of the sky scenery as well as that of
the woods and meadows and rushy, lily-bordered lakes. The
great thunder-storms in particular interested us, so unlike any
seen in Scotland, exciting awful, wondering admiration. Gazing awe-stricken, we watched the upbuilding of the sublime
cloud-mountains – glowing, sun-beaten pearl and alabaster
cumuli, glorious in beauty and majesty and looking so firm
and lasting that birds, we thought, might build their nests amid
their downy bosses; the black-browed storm-clouds marching
in awful grandeur across the landscape, trailing broad gray
sheets of hail and rain like vast cataracts, and ever and anon
gashing down vivid zigzag lightning followed by terrible
crashing thunder. We saw several trees shattered, and one
of them, a punky old oak, was set on fire, while we wondered
why all the trees and everybody and everything did not share
the same fate, for oftentimes the whole sky blazed. After sultry
storm days, many of the nights were darkened by smooth
black apparently structureless cloud-mantles which at short
intervals were illumined with startling suddenness to a fiery
glow by quick, quivering lightning-flashes, revealing the landscape in almost noonday brightness, to be instantly quenched
in solid blackness.

But those first days and weeks of unmixed enjoyment and
freedom, reveling in the wonderful wildness about us, were

soon to be mingled with the hard work of making a farm. I was first put to burning brush in clearing land for the plough. Those magnificent brush fires with great white hearts and red flames, the first big, wild outdoor fires I had ever seen, were wonderful sights for young eyes. Again and again, when they were burning fiercest so that we could hardly approach near enough to throw on another branch, Father put them to awfully practical use as warning lessons, comparing their heat with that of hell, and the branches with bad boys. 'Now, John,' he would say – 'now, John, just think what an awful thing it would be to be thrown into that fire – and then think of hell-fire, that is so many times hotter. Into that fire all bad boys, with sinners of every sort who disobey God, will be cast as we are casting branches into this brush fire, and although suffering so much, their sufferings will never, never end, because neither the fire nor the sinners can die.' But those terrible fire lessons quickly faded away in the blithe wilderness air; for no fire can be hotter than the heavenly fire of faith and hope that burns in every healthy boy's heart.

Soon after our arrival in the woods someone added a cat and puppy to the animals Father had bought. The cat soon had kittens, and it was interesting to watch her feeding, protecting, and training them. After they were able to leave their nest and play, she went out hunting and brought in many kinds of birds and squirrels for them, mostly ground squirrels (spermophiles), called 'gophers' in Wisconsin. When she got within a dozen yards or so of the shanty, she announced her approach by a peculiar call, and the sleeping kittens immediately bounced up and ran to meet her, all racing for the first bite of they knew not what, and we too ran to see what she brought. She then lay down a few minutes to rest and enjoy the enjoyment of her feasting family, and again vanished in the grass and flowers, coming and going every half-hour or so. Sometimes she brought in birds that we had never seen before, and occasionally a flying squirrel, chipmunk, or big fox squirrel. We were just old enough, David and I, to regard all these creatures as wonders, the strange inhabitants of our new world.

The pup was a common cur, though very uncommon to us, a black and white short-haired mongrel that we named 'Watch.' We always gave him a pan of milk in the evening just before we knelt in family worship, while daylight still lingered in the shanty. And, instead of attending to the prayers, I too often studied the small wild creatures playing around us. Field mice scampered about the cabin as though it had been built for them alone, and their performances were very amusing. About dusk, on one of the calm, sultry nights so grateful to moths and beetles, when the puppy was lapping his milk, and we were on our knees, in through the door came a heavy broad-shouldered beetle about as big as a mouse, and after it had droned and boomed round the cabin two or three times, the pan of milk, showing white in the gloaming, caught its eyes, and, taking good aim, it alighted with a slanting, glinting plash in the middle of the pan like a duck alighting in a lake. Baby Watch, having never before seen anything like that beetle, started back, gazing in dumb astonishment and fear at the black sprawling monster trying to swim. Recovering somewhat from his fright, he began to bark at the creature, and ran round and round his milk pan, wouf-woufing, gurring, growling, like an old dog barking at a wild-cat or a bear. The natural aston-ishment and curiosity of that boy dog getting his first ento-mological lesson in this wonderful world was so immoderately funny that I had great difficulty in keeping from laughing out loud.

Snapping turtles were common throughout the woods, and we were delighted to find that they would snap at a stick and hang on like bull-dogs; and we amused ourselves by introdu-cing Watch to them, enjoying his curious behavior and theirs in getting acquainted with each other. One day we assisted one of the smallest of the turtles to get a good grip of poor Watch's ear. Then away he rushed, holding his head sidewise, yelping and terror-stricken, with the strange buglike reptile biting hard and clinging fast – a shameful amusement even for wild boys.

As a playmate Watch was too serious, though he learned more than any stranger would judge him capable of, was a bold, faithful watch-dog, and in his prime a grand fighter, able to whip all the other dogs in the neighborhood. Comparing him with ourselves, we soon learned that although he could not read books he could read faces, was a good judge of character, always knew what was going on and what we were about to do, and liked to help us. We could run nearly as fast as he could, see about as far and perhaps hear as well, but in sense of smell his nose was incomparably better than ours. One sharp winter morning when the ground was covered with snow, I noticed that when he was yawning and stretching himself after leaving his bed he suddenly caught the scent of something that excited him, went round the corner of the house, and looked intently to the westward across a tongue of land that we called West Bank, eagerly questioning the air with quivering nostrils, and bristling up as though he felt sure that there was something dangerous in that direction and had actually caught sight of it. Then he ran toward the Bank, and I followed him, curious to see what his nose had discovered. The top of the Bank commanded a view of the north end of our lake and meadow, and when we got there we saw an Indian hunter with a long spear, going from one muskrat cabin to another, approaching cautiously, careful to make no noise, and then suddenly thrusting his spear down through the house. If well aimed, the spear went through the poor beaver rat as it lay cuddled up in the snug nest it had made for itself in the fall with so much far-seeing care, and when the hunter felt the spear quivering, he dug down the mossy hut with his tomahawk and secured his prey – the flesh for food, and the skin to sell for a dime or so. This was a clear object lesson on dogs' keenness of scent. That Indian was more than half a mile away across a wooded ridge. Had the hunter been a white man, I suppose Watch would not have noticed him.

When he was about six or seven years old, he not only became cross, so that he would do only what he liked, but he fell on evil ways, and was accused by the neighbors who had settled around us of catching and devouring whole broods of chickens, some of them only a day or two out of the shell. We never imagined he would do anything so grossly undoglike. He never did at home. But several of the neighbors declared over and over again that they had caught him in the act, and insisted that he must be shot. At last, in spite of tearful protests, he was condemned and executed. Father examined the poor fellow's stomach in search of sure evidence, and discovered the heads of eight chickens that he had devoured at his last meal. So poor Watch was killed simply because his taste for chickens was too much like our own. Think of the millions of squabs that preaching, praying men and women kill and eat, with all sorts of other animals great and small, young and old, while eloquently discoursing on the coming of the blessed peaceful, bloodless millennium! Think of the passenger pigeons that fifty or sixty years ago filled the woods and sky over half the continent, now exterminated by beating down the young from the nests together with the brooding parents, before they could try their wonderful wings; by trapping them in nets, feeding them to hogs, etc. None of our fellow mortals is safe who eats what we eat, who in any way interferes with our pleasures, or who may be used for work or food, clothing or ornament, or mere cruel, sportish amusement. Fortunately many are too small to be seen, and therefore enjoy life beyond our reach. And in looking through God's great stone books made up of records reaching back millions and millions of years, it is a great comfort to learn that vast multitudes of creatures, great and small and infinite in number, lived and had a good time in God's lose before man was created.

The old Scotch fashion of whipping for every act of disobedience or of simple, playful forgetfulness was still kept up in the wilderness, and of course many of those whippings fell upon me. Most of them were outrageously severe, and utterly barren of fun. But here is one that was nearly all fun.

Father was busy hauling lumber for the frame house that was to be got ready for the arrival of my mother, sisters, and brother, left behind in Scotland. One morning, when he was ready to start for another load, his ox-whip was not to be found. He asked me if I knew anything about it. I told him I didn't know where it was, but Scotch conscience compelled me to confess that when I was playing with it I had tied it to Watch's tail, and that he ran away, dragging it through the grass, and came back without it. 'It must have slipped off his tail,' I said, and so I didn't know where it was. This honest, straightforward little story made Father so angry that he exclaimed with heavy, foreboding emphasis: 'The very deevil's in that boy!' David, who had been playing with me and was perhaps about as responsible for the loss of the whip as I was, said never a word, for he was always prudent enough to hold his tongue when the parental weather was stormy, and so escaped nearly all punishment. And, strange to say, this time I also escaped, all except a terrible scolding, though the thrashing weather seemed darker than ever. As if unwilling to let the sun see the shameful job, Father took me into the cabin where the storm was to fall, and sent David to the woods for a switch. While he was out selecting the switch, Father put in the spare time sketching my play-wickedness in awful colors, and of course referred again and again to the place prepared for bad boys. In the midst of this terrible word-storm, dreading most the impending thrashing, I whimpered that I was only playing because I couldn't help it; didn't know I was doing wrong; wouldn't do it again, and so forth. After this miserable dialogue was about exhausted, Father became impatient at my brother for taking so long to find the switch; and so was I, for I wanted to have the thing over and done with. At last, in came David, a picture of open-hearted innocence, solemnly dragging a young bur-oak sapling, and handed the end of it to Father, saying it was the best switch he could find. It was an awfully heavy one, about two and a half inches thick at the butt and ten feet long, almost big enough for a fence-pole. There wasn't room enough in the cabin to swing it, and the moment I saw it I burst out laughing in the midst of my fears. But Father failed to see the fun and was very angry at David, heaved the bur-oak outside and passionately demanded his reason for fetching 'sic a muckle rail like that instead o' a switch? Do ye ca' that a switch? I have a gude mind to thrash you instead o' John.' David, with demure, downcast eyes, looked preternaturally righteous, but as usual prudently answered never a word.

It was a hard job in those days to bring up Scotch boys in the way they should go; and poor overworked Father was determined to do it if enough of the right kind of switches could be found. But this time, as the sun was getting high, he hitched up old Tom and Jerry and made haste to the Kingston lumber-yard, leaving me unscathed and as innocently wicked as ever; for hardly had Father got fairly out of sight among the oaks and hickories, ere all our troubles, hell-threatenings, and exhortations were forgotten in the fun we had lassoing a stubborn old sow and laboriously trying to teach her to go reasonably steady in rope harness. She was the first hog that Father bought to stock the farm, and we boys regarded her as a very wonderful beast. In a few weeks she had a lot of pigs, and of all the queer, funny, animal children we had yet seen, none aroused us more. They were so comic in size and shape, in their gait and gestures, their merry sham fights, and the false alarms they got up for the fun of scampering back to their mother and begging her in most persuasive little squeals to lie down and give them a drink.

After her darling short-snouted babies were about a month old, she took them out to the woods and gradually roamed farther and farther from the shanty in search of acorns and roots. One afternoon we heard a rifle-shot, a very noticeable thing, as we had no near neighbors, as yet. We thought it must have been fired by an Indian on the trail that followed the right bank of the Fox River between Portage and Packwaukee Lake and passed our shanty at a distance of about three quarters of a mile. Just a few minutes after that shot was heard along came the poor mother rushing up to the shanty for protection, with her pigs, all out of breath and terror-stricken. One of them was missing, and we supposed of course that an Indian had shot it for food. Next day, I discovered a blood-puddle where the Indian trail crossed the outlet of our lake. One of Father's hired men told us that the Indians thought nothing of levying this sort of blackmail whenever they were hungry. The solemn awe and fear in the eyes of that old mother and those little pigs I never can forget; it was as unmistakable and deadly a fear as I ever saw expressed by any human eye, and corroborates in no uncertain way the oneness of all of us.

Chapter 3

LIFE ON A WISCONSIN FARM

Coming direct from school in Scotland while we were still hopefully ignorant and far from tame – notwithstanding the unnatural profusion of teaching and thrashing lavished upon us – getting acquainted with the animals about us was a never-failing source of wonder and delight. At first my father, like nearly all the backwoods settlers, bought a yoke of oxen to do the farm work, and as field after field was cleared, the number was gradually increased until we had five yoke. These wise, patient, plodding animals did all the ploughing, logging, hauling, and hard work of every sort for the first four or five years, and, never having seen oxen before, we looked at them with the same eager freshness of conception as we did at the wild animals. We worked with them, sympathized with them in their rest and toil and play, and thus learned to know them far better than we should hail we been only trained scientific naturalists. We soon learned that each ox and cow and calf had individual character. Old white-faced Buck, one of the second yoke of oxen we owned, was a notably sagacious fellow. He seemed to reason sometimes almost like ourselves. In the fall we fed the cattle lots of pumpkins and had to split them open so that mouthfuls could be readily broken off. But Buck never waited for us to come to his help. The others, when they were hungry and impatient, tried to break through the hard rind with their teeth, but seldom with success if the pumpkin was full grown. Buck never wasted time in this mumbling, slavering way, but crushed them with his head. He went to the pile, picked out a good one, like a boy choosing an orange or apple, rolled it down on to the open ground, deliberately kneeled in front of it, placed his broad, flat brow on top of it, brought his weight hard down and crushed it, then quietly arose and went on with his meal in comfort. Some would call this 'instinct,' as if so-called 'blind instinct' must necessarily make an ox stand on its head to break pumpkins when its teeth got sore, or when nobody came with an axe to split them. Another fine ox showed his skill when hungry by opening all the fences that stood in his way to the corn-fields.

The humanity we found in them came partly through the expression of their eyes when tired, their tones of voice when hungry and calling for food, their patient plodding and pulling in hot weather, their long-drawn-out sighing breath when exhausted and suffering like ourselves, and their enjoyment of rest with the same grateful looks as ours. We recognized their kinship also by their yawning like ourselves when sleepy and evidently enjoying the same peculiar pleasure at the roots of their jaws; by the way they stretched themselves in the morning after a good rest; by learning languages – Scotch, English, Irish, French, Dutch – a smattering of each as required in the faithful service they so willingly, wisely rendered; by their intelligent, alert curiosity, manifested in listening to strange sounds; their love of play; the attachments they made; and their mourning, long continued, when a companion was killed.

When we went to Portage, our nearest town, about ten or twelve miles from the farm, it would oftentimes be late before we got back, and in the summer-time, in sultry, rainy weather, the clouds were full of sheet lightning which every minute or two would suddenly illumine the landscape, revealing all its features, the hills and valleys, meadows and trees, about as fully and clearly as the noonday sunshine; then as suddenly the glorious light would be quenched, making the darkness seem denser than before. On such nights the cattle had to find the way home without any help from us, but they never got off the track, for they followed it by scent like dogs. Once, Father, returning late from Portage or Kingston, compelled Tom and

Jerry, our first oxen, to leave the dim track, imagining they must be going wrong. At last they stopped and refused to go farther. Then Father unhitched them from the wagon, took hold of Tom's tail, and was thus led straight to the shanty. Next morning he set out to seek his wagon and found it on the brow of a steep hill above an impassable swamp. We learned less from the cows, because we did not enter so far into their lives, working with them, suffering heat and cold, hunger and thirst, and almost deadly weariness with them; but none with natural charity could fail to sympathize with them in their love for their calves, and to feel that it in no way differed from the divine mother-love of a woman in thoughtful, self-sacrificing care; for they would brave every danger, giving their lives for their off-spring. Nor could we fail to sympathize with their awkward, blunt-nosed baby calves, with such beautiful, wondering eyes looking out on the world and slowly getting acquainted with things, all so strange to them, and awkwardly learning to use their legs, and play and fight.

Before leaving Scotland, Father promised us a pony to ride when we got to America, and we saw to it that this promise was not forgotten. Only a week or two after our arrival in the woods he bought us a little Indian pony for thirteen dollars from a store-keeper in Kingston who had obtained him from a Winnebago or Menominee Indian in trade for goods. He was a stout handsome bay with long black mane and tail, and, though he was only two years old, the Indians had already taught him to carry all sorts of burdens, to stand without being tied, to go anywhere over all sorts of ground fast or slow, and to jump and swim and fear nothing – a truly wonderful creature, strangely different from shy, skittish, nervous, superstitious civilized beasts. We turned him loose, and, strange to say, he never ran away from us or refused to be caught, but behaved as if he had known Scotch boys all his life, probably because we were about as wild as young Indians.

One day when Father happened to have a little leisure, he said, 'Noo, bairns, rin doon the meadow and get your powny and learn to ride him.' So we led him out to a smooth place near an Indian mound back of the shanty, where Father directed us to begin. I mounted for the first memorable lesson, crossed the mound, and set out at a slow walk along the wagon-track made in hauling lumber; then Father shouted: 'Whup him up, John, whup him up! Make him gallop; gallopin' is easier and better than walkin' or trottin'.' Jack was willing, and away he sped at a good fast gallop. I managed to keep my balance fairly well by holding fast to the mane, but could not keep from bumping up and down, for I was plump and elastic and so was Jack; therefore about half of the time I was in the air.

After a quarter of a mile or so of this curious transportation, I cried, 'Whoa, Jack!' The wonderful creature seemed to understand Scotch, for he stopped so suddenly I flew over his head, but he stood perfectly still as if that flying method of dismounting were the regular way. Jumping on again, I bumped and bobbed back along the grassy, flowery track, over the Indian mound, cried, 'Whoa, Jack!' flew over his head, and alighted in Father's arms as gracefully as if it were all intended for circus work.

After going over the course five or six times in the same free, picturesque style, I gave place to brother David, whose performances were much like my own. In a few weeks, however, or a month, we were taking adventurous rides more than a mile long out to a big meadow frequented by sandhill cranes, and returning safely with wonderful stories of the great long-legged birds we had seen, and how on the whole journey away and back we had fallen off only five or six times. Gradually we learned to gallop through the woods without roads of any sort, bareback and without rope or bridle, guiding only by leaning from side to side or by slight knee pressure. In this free way we used to amuse ourselves, tilting at full speed across a big 'kettle' that was on our farm, without holding on by either mane or tail.

These so-called 'kettles' were formed by the melting of large detached blocks of ice that had been buried in moraine material thousands of years ago when the ice-sheet that covered all this region was receding. As the buried ice melted, of course the moraine material above and about it fell in, forming hopper-shaped hollows, while the grass growing on their sides and around them prevented the rain and wind from filling them up. The one we performed in was perhaps seventy or eighty feet wide and twenty or thirty feet deep; and without a saddle or hold of any kind it was not easy to keep from slipping over Jack's head in diving into it, or over his tail climbing out. This was fine sport on the long summer Sundays when we were able to steal away before meeting-time without being seen. We got very warm and red at it, and oftentimes poor Jack, dripping with sweat like his riders, seemed to have been boiled in that kettle.

In Scotland we had often been admonished to be bold, and this advice we passed on to Jack, who had already got many a wild lesson from Indian boys. Once, when teaching him to jump muddy streams, I made him try the creek in our meadow at a place where it is about twelve feet wide. He jumped bravely enough, but came down with a grand splash hardly more than halfway over. The water was only about a foot in depth, but the black vegetable mud half afloat was unfathomable I managed to wallow ashore, but poor Jack sank deeper and deeper until only his head was visible in the black abyss, and his Indian fortitude was desperately tried. His foundering so suddenly in the treacherous gulf recalled the story of the Abbot of Aberbrothok's bell, which went down with a gurgling sound while bubbles rose and burst around. I had to go to Father for help. He tied a long hemp rope brought from Scotland around Jack's neck, and Tom and Jerry seemed to have all they could do to pull him out. After which I got a solemn scolding for asking the 'puir beast to jump intil sic a saft bottomless place.'

We moved into our frame house in the fall, when Mother with the rest of the family arrived from Scotland, and, when the winter snow began to fly, the bur-oak shanty was made into a stable for Jack. Father told us that good meadow hay was all he required, but we fed him corn, lots of it, and he grew very frisky and fat. About the middle of winter his long hair was full of dust and, as we thought, required washing. So, without taking the frosty weather into account, we gave him a thorough soap and water scouring, and as we failed to get him rubbed dry, a row of icicles formed under his belly. Father happened to see him in this condition and angrily asked what we had been about. We said Jack was dirty and we had washed him to make him healthy. He told us we ought to be ashamed of ourselves, 'soaking the puir beast in cauld water at this time o' year'; that when we wanted to clean him we should have sense enough to use the brush and curry-comb.

In summer Dave or I had to ride after the cows every evening about sundown, and Jack got so accustomed to bringing in the drove that when we happened to be a few minutes late he used to go off alone at the regular time and bring them home at a gallop. It used to make Father very angry to see Jack chasing the cows like a shepherd dog, running from one to the other and giving each a bite on the rump to keep them on the run, flying before him as if pursued by wolves. Father would declare at times that the wicked beast had the deevil in him and would be the death of the cattle. The corral and barn were just at the foot of a hill, and he made a great display of the drove on the home stretch as they walloped down that hill with their tails on end.

One evening when the pell-mell Wild West show was at its wildest, it made Father so extravagantly mad that he ordered me to 'Shoot Jack!' I went to the house and brought the gun, suffering most horrible mental anguish, such as I suppose unhappy Abraham felt when commanded to slay Isaac. Jack's life was spared, however, though I can't tell what finally became of him. I wish I could. After Father bought a span of work horses he was sold to a man who said he was going to ride him across the plains to California. We had him, I think, some five or six years. He was the stoutest, gentlest, bravest little horse I ever saw. He never seemed tired, could canter all day with a man about as heavy as himself on his back, and feared nothing. Once fifty or sixty pounds of beef that was tied on his back slid over his shoulders along his neck and weighed down his head to the ground, fairly anchoring him; but he stood patient and still for half an hour or so without making the slightest struggle to free himself, while I was away getting help to untie the pack-rope and set the load back in its place.

As I was the eldest boy I had the care of our first span of work horses. Their names were Nob and Nell. Nob was very intelligent, and even affectionate, and could learn almost anything. Nell was entirely different; balky and stubborn, though we managed to teach her a good many circus tricks; but she never seemed to like to play with us in anything like an affectionate way as Nob did. We turned them out one day into the pasture, and an Indian, hiding in the brush that had sprung up after the grass fires had been kept out, managed to catch Nob, tied a rope to her jaw for a bridle, rode her to Green Lake, about thirty or forty miles away, and tried to sell her for fifteen dollars. All our hearts were sore, as if one of the family had been lost. We hunted everywhere and could not at first imagine what had become of her. We discovered her track where the fence was broken down, and, following it for a few miles, made sure the track was Nob's; and a neighbor told us he had seen an Indian riding fast through the woods on a horse that looked like Nob. But we could find no farther trace of her until a month or two after she was lost, and we had given up hope of ever seeing her again. Then we learned that she had been taken from an Indian by a farmer at Green Lake because he saw that she had been shod and had worked in harness. So when the Indian tried to sell her the farmer said: 'You are a thief. That is a white man's horse. You stole her.'

'No,' said the Indian, 'I brought her from Prairie du Chien and she has always been mine.'

The man, pointing to her feet and the marks of the harness, said: 'You are lying. I will take that horse away from you and put her in my pasture, and if you come near it I will set the dogs on you.' Then he advertized her. One of our neighbors happened to see the advertisement and brought us the glad news, and great was our rejoicing when Father brought her home. That Indian must have treated her with terrible cruelty, for when I was riding her through the pasture several years afterward, looking for another horse that we wanted to catch, as we approached the place where she had been captured she stood stock still gazing through the bushes, fearing the Indian might still be hiding there ready to spring; and she was so excited that she trembled, and her heartbeats were so loud that I could hear them distinctly as I sat on her back, *boomp*, *boomp*, *boomp*, like the drumming of a partridge. So vividly had she remembered her terrible experiences.

She was a great pet and favorite with the whole family, quickly learned playful tricks, came running when we called, seemed to know everything we said to her, and had the utmost confidence in our friendly kindness.

We used to cut and shock and husk the Indian corn in the fall, until a keen Yankee stopped overnight at our house and among other laboursaving notions convinced Father that it was better to let it stand, and husk it at his leisure during the winter, then turn in the cattle to eat the leaves and trample down the stalks, so that they could be ploughed under in the spring. In this winter method each of us took two rows and husked into baskets, and emptied the corn on the ground in piles of fifteen to twenty basketfuls, then loaded it into the wagon to be hauled to the crib. This was cold, painful work, the temperature being oftentimes far below zero and the ground covered with dry, frosty snow, giving rise to miserable crops of chilblains and frosted fingers – a sad change from the merry Indian-summer husking, when the big yellow pumpkins covered the cleared fields – golden corn, golden pumpkins, gathered in the hazy golden weather. Sad change, indeed, but we occasionally got some fun out of the nipping, shivery work from hungry prairie chickens, and squirrels and mice that came about us.

The piles of corn were often left in the field several days, and while loading them into the wagon we usually found field mice in them – big, blunt-nosed, strong-scented fellows that we were taught to kill just because they nibbled a few grains of corn. I used to hold one while it was still warm, up to Nob's nose for the fun of seeing her make faces and snort at the smell of it; and I would say: 'Here, Nob,' as if offering her a lump of sugar. One day I offered her an extra fine, fat, pomp specimen, something like a little woodchuck, or muskrat, and to my astonishment, after smelling it curiously and doubtfully, as if wondering what the gift might be, and rubbing it back and forth in the palm of my hand with her upper lip, she deliberately took it into her mouth, crunched and munched and chewed it fine and swallowed it, bones, teeth, head, tail, everything. Not a single hair of that mouse was wasted. When she was chewing it she nodded and grunted, as though critically tasting and relishing it.

My father was a steadfast enthusiast on religious matters, and, of course, attended almost every sort of church-meeting, especially revival meetings. They were occasionally held in summer, but mostly in winter when the sleighing was good and plenty of time available. One hot summer day Father drove Nob to Portage and back, twenty-four miles over a sandy road. It was a hot, hard, sultry day's work, and she had evidently been over driven in order to get home in time for one of these meetings. I shall never forget how tired and wilted she looked that evening when I unhitched her; how she drooped in her stall, too tired to eat or even to lie down. Next morning it was plain that her lungs were inflamed; all the dreadful symptoms were just the same as my own when I had pneumonia Father sent for a Methodist minister, a very energetic, resourceful man, who was a blacksmith, farmer, butcher, and horse-doctor as well as minister; but all his gifts and skill were of no avail. Nob was doomed. We bathed her head and tried to get her to eat something, but she couldn't eat, and in about a couple of weeks we turned her loose to let her come around the house and see us in the weary suffering and loneliness of the shadow of death. She tried to follow us children, so long her friends and workmates and playmates. It was awfully touching. She had several hemorrhages, and in the forenoon of her last day, after she had had one of her dreadful spells of bleeding and gasping for breath, she came to me trembling, with beseeching, heartbreaking looks, and after I had bathed her head and tried to soothe and pet her, she lay down and gasped and died. All the family gathered about her, weeping, with aching hearts. Then dust to dust.

She was the most faithful, intelligent, playful, affectionate, human-like horse I ever knew, and she won all our hearts. Of the many advantages of farm life for boys one of the greatest is the gaining a real knowledge of animals as fellow-mortals, learning to respect them and love them, and even to win some of their love. Thus Godlike sympathy grows and thrives and spreads far beyond the teachings of churches and schools, where too often the mean, blinding, loveless doctrine is taught that animals have neither mind nor soul, have no rights that we are bound to respect, and were made only for man, to be petted, spoiled, slaughtered, or enslaved.

At first we were afraid of snakes, but soon learned that most of them were harmless. The only venomous species seen on our farm were the rattlesnake and the copperhead, one of each. David saw the rattler, and we both saw the copperhead. One day, when my brother came in from his work, he reported that he had seen a snake that made a queer buzzy noise with its tail. This was the only rattlesnake seen on our farm, though we heard of them being common on limestone hills eight or ten miles distant. We discovered the copperhead when we were ploughing, and we saw and felt at the first long, fixed, half-charmed, admiring stare at him that he was an awfully dangerous fellow. Every fiber of his strong, lithe, quivering body, his burnished copper-colored head, and above all his fierce, able eyes, seemed to be overflowing full of deadly power, and bade us beware. And yet it is only fair to say that this terrible, beautiful reptile showed no disposition to hurt us until we threw clods at him and tried to head him off from a log fence into which he was trying to escape. We were barefooted and of course afraid to let him get very near, while we vainly battered him with the loose sandy clods of the freshly ploughed field to hold him back until we could get a stick. Looking us in the eyes after a moment's pause, he probably saw we were afraid, and he came right straight at us, snapping and looking terrible, drove us out of his way, and won his fight.

Out on the open sandy hills there were a good many thick burly blow snakes, the kind that puff themselves up and hiss. Our Yankee declared that their breath was very poisonous and that we must not go near them. A handsome ringed species common in damp, shady places was, he told us, the most wonderful of all the snakes, for if chopped into pieces, however small, the fragments would wriggle themselves together again, and the restored snake would go on about its business as if nothing had happened. The commonest kinds were the striped slender species of the meadows and streams, good swimmers, that lived mostly on frogs.

Once I observed one of the larger ones, about two feet long, pursuing a frog in our meadow, and it was wonderful to see how fast the legless, footless, wingless, finless hunter could run. The frog, of course, knew its enemy and was making desperate efforts to escape to the water and hide in the marsh mud. He was a fine, sleek yellow muscular fellow and was springing over the tall grass in wide-arching jumps. The green-striped snake, gliding swiftly and steadily, was keeping the frog in sight and, had I not interfered, would probably have tired out the poor jumper. Then, perhaps, while digesting and enjoying his meal, the happy snake would himself be swallowed, frog and all, by a hawk. Again, to our astonishment, the small specimens were attacked by our hens. They pursued and pecked away at them until they killed and devoured them, oftentimes quarreling over the division of the spoil, though it was not easily divided.

We watched the habits of the swift-darting dragonflies, wild bees, butterflies, wasps, beetles, etc., and soon learned to discriminate between those that might be safely handled and the pinching or stinging species. But of all our wild neighbors the mosquitoes were the first with which we became very intimately acquainted.

The beautiful in the spring meadow lying warm sunshine,

outspread between our lily-rimmed lake and the hill-slope that our shanty stood on, sent forth thirsty swans of the little gray, speckledy, singing, stinging pests; and how tellingly they introduced themselves! Of little avail were the smudges that we made on muggy evenings to drive them away; and amid the many lessons which they insisted upon teaching us we wondered more and more at the extent of their knowledge, especially that in their tiny, flimsy bodies room could be found for such cunning palates. They would drink their fill from brown, smoky Indians, or from old white folk flavored with tobacco and whiskey, when no better could be had. But the surpassing fineness of their taste was best manifested by their enthusiastic appreciation of boys full of lively red blood, and of girls in full bloom fresh from cool Scotland or England. On these it was pleasant to witness their enjoyment as they feasted. Indians, we were told, believed that if they were brave fighters they would go after death to a happy country abounding in game, where there were no mosquitoes and no cowards. For cowards were driven away by themselves to a miserable country where there was no game fit to eat, and where the sky was always dark with huge gnats and mosquitoes as big as pigeons.

We were great admirers of the little black water-bugs. Their whole lives seemed to be play, skimming, swimming, swirling, and waltzing together in little groups on the edge of the lake and in the meadow springs, dancing to music we never could hear. The long-legged skaters, too, seemed wonderful fellows, shuffling about on top of the water, with air-bubbles like little bladders tangled under their hairy feet; and we often wished that we also might be shod in the same way to enable us to skate on the lake in summer as well as in icy winter. Not less wonderful were the boatmen, swimming on their backs, pulling themselves along with a pair of oar-like legs.

Great was the delight of brothers David and Daniel and myself when Father gave us a few pine boards for a boat, and it was a memorable day when we got that boat built and launched into the lake. Never shall I forget our first sail over the gradually deepening water, the sun-beams pouring through it revealing the strange plants covering the bottom, and the fishes coming about us, staring and wondering as if the boat were a monstrous strange fish.

The water was so clear that it was almost invisible, and when we floated slowly out over the plants and fishes, we seemed to be miraculously sustained in the air while silently exploring a veritable fairyland.

We always had to work hard, but if we worked still harder we were occasionally allowed a little spell in the long summer evenings about sundown to fish, and on Sundays an hour or two to sail quietly without fishing-rod or gun when the lake was calm. Therefore we gradually learned something about its inhabitants – pickerel, sunfish, black bass, perch, shiners, pumpkin-seeds, ducks, loons, turtles, muskrats, etc. We saw the sunfishes making their nests in little openings in the rushes where the water was only a few feet deep, ploughing up and shoving away the soft gray mud with their noses, like pigs, forming round bowls five or six inches in depth and about two feet in diameter, in which their eggs were deposited. And with what beautiful, unweariable devotion they watched and hovered over them and chased away prowling spawn-eating enemies that ventured within a rod or two of the precious nest!

The pickerel is a savage fish endowed with marvelous strength and speed. It lies in wait for its prey on the bottom, perfectly motionless like a waterlogged stick, watching everything that moves, with fierce, hungry eyes. Oftentimes when we were fishing for some other kinds over the edge of the boat, a pickerel that we had not noticed would come like a bolt of lightning and seize the fish we had caught before we could get it into the boat. The very first pickerel that I ever caught jumped into the air to seize a small fish dangling on my line, and, missing its aim, fell plump into the boat as if it had dropped from the sky.

Some of our neighbors fished for pickerel through the ice in midwinter. They usually drove a wagon out on the lake, set a large number of lines baited with live minnows, hung a loop of

John Muir's childhood home. This image from Muir's own collection shows his childhood home as it was just before his only return to Dunbar in 1893. (Copyright © Muir-Hanna Trust.)

View of Victorian Dunbar. By 1914 Muir's Grammar School was hidden within a larger complex. This earlier view of the town from the church tower shows Muir's school on the right. (Copyright © Muir-Hanna Trust.)

The young John Muir. Few early photographs of John Muir exist:
Father frowned on non-Biblical innovations and 'graven images'.
(Copyright © Wisconsin Historical Society.)

John Muir's desk clock. 'An Ingenious Whittler'. Muir's desk clock survives with the Wisconsin State Historical Society in Madison. Muir was able to parley his early experiments in technology and his Dunbar Grammar School education into a university place. His subsequent constructions became a wonder of the campus. (Copyright © Wisconsin Historical Society)

Drawing of John Muir's desk clock. Muir's own drawing of his desk clock complements the physical artefact. Many more drawings than objects have survived, providing a good indication of the range of Muir's inventiveness. (Copyright © Wisconsin Historical Society.)

The Fountain Lake Farmhouse. The Muir family home at the new Fountain Lake farm was built by the autumn of their first year in America, ready for the arrival of the rest of the family. With eight rooms, it served the family for just eight years. (Copyright © Wisconsin Historical Society.)

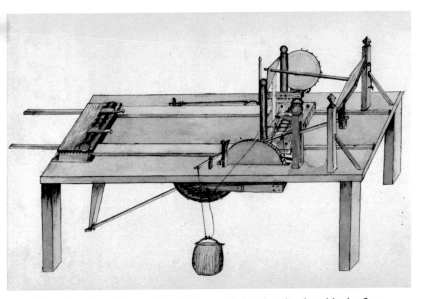

Drawing of a table saw. The table saw in this drawing heralds the first phase of Muir's life after leaving university when he supported himself as a technologist. (Copyright © Wisconsin Historical Society.)

Drawing of University Hall by D.C. Salisbury. The University of Wisconsin was founded in 1848. When Muir began his course of study he roomed in the 1851-built North Hall, one of the three original University buildings shown in this early drawing. (Copyright © Wisconsin Historical Society.)

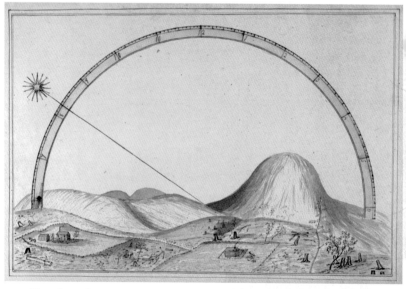

Drawing of a clock. John Muir drew this 'star clock' around 1863 before he began his life-long explorations; perhaps he was already thinking of practical (and impractical) means of surviving in the wilderness? (Copyright © Wisconsin Historical Society.)

Broxburn Smithy. This photograph by Thomas Bissett was prized by
John Muir as the 'site of the Battle of Dunbar'; Broxburn Smithy
was just one of many such establishments in and around Dunbar.
(Courtesy of David M. Anderson.)

Stormy seas. Thomas Bisset was expert in capturing the very worst
of the 'stormy North Sea'. Muir owned a copy of this photograph
showing Dunbar's 18th-century defensive battery being bombarded
by towering waves. (Courtesy of David M. Anderson.)

Off to the herring, photographed by Thomas Bisset. Perhaps John Muir treasured this image because he remembered watching the boats leaving harbour on these long ago days when he was still a boy in Dunbar. (Courtesy of David M. Anderson.)

the lines over a small bush planted at the side of each hole, and watched to see the loops pulled off when a fish had taken the bait. Large quantities of pickerel were often caught in this cruel way.

Our beautiful lake, named Fountain Lake by Father, but Muir's Lake by the neighbors, is one of the many small glacier lakes that adorn the Wisconsin landscapes. It is fed by twenty or thirty meadow springs about half a mile long, half as wide, and surrounded by low finely modeled hills dotted with oak and hickory, and meadows full of grasses and sedges and many beautiful orchids and ferns. First there is a zone of green, shining rushes, and just beyond the rushes a zone of white and orange water-lilies fifty or sixty feet wide forming a magnificent border. On bright days, when the lake was rippled by a breeze, the lilies and sun-spangles danced together in radiant beauty, and it became difficult to discriminate between them.

On Sundays, after or before chores and sermons and Bible-lessons, we drifted about on the lake for hours, especially in lily time, getting finest lessons and sermons from the water and flowers, ducks, fishes, and muskrats. In particular we took Christ's advice and devoutly 'considered the lilies' – how they grow up in beauty out of gray lime mud, and ride gloriously among the breezy sun-spangles. On our way home we gathered grand bouquets of them to be kept fresh all the week. No flower was hailed with greater wonder and admiration by the European settlers in general – Scotch, English, and Irish – than this white water-lily (*Nymphoea odorata*). It is a magnificent plant, queen of the inland waters, pure white, three or four inches in diameter, the most beautiful, sumptuous and deliciously fragrant of all our Wisconsin flowers. No lily garden in civilization we had ever seen could compare with our lake garden.

The next most admirable flower in the estimation of settlers in this part of the new world was the pasque-flower or wind-flower (*Anemone Patens* var. *Nuttalliana*). It is the very first to appear in the spring, covering the cold gray-black ground with

cheery blossoms. Before the axe or plough had touched the
'oak openings' of Wisconsin, they were swept by running fires
almost every autumn after the grass became dry. If from any
cause, such as early snowstorms or late rains, they happened to
escape the autumn fire besom, they were likely to be burned in
the spring after the snow melted. But whether burned in the
spring or fall, ashes and bits of charred twigs and grass stems
made the whole country look dismal. Then, before a single
grass-blade had sprouted, a hopeful multitude of large hairy,
silky buds about as thick as one's thumb came to light, pushing
up through the black and gray ashes and cinders, and before
these buds were fairly free from the ground they opened wide
and displayed purple blossoms about two inches in diameter,
giving beauty for ashes in glorious abundance. Instead of
remaining in the ground waiting for warm weather and
companions, this admirable plant seemed to be in haste to
rise and cheer the desolate landscape. Then at its leisure, after
other plants had come to its help, it spread its leaves and grew
up to a height of about two or three feet. The spreading leaves
formed a whorl on the ground, and another about the middle
of the stem as an involucre, and on the top of the stem the silky,
hairy long-tailed seeds formed a head like a second flower. A
little church was established among the earlier settlers and the
meetings at first were held in our house. After working hard all
the week it was difficult for boys to sit still through long
sermons without falling asleep, especially in warm weather. In
this drowsy trouble the charming anemone came to our help. A
pocketful of the pungent seeds industriously nibbled while the
discourses were at their dullest kept us awake and filled our
minds with flowers.

The next great flower wonders on which we lavished admiration, not only for beauty of color and size, but for their
curious shapes, were the cypripediums, called 'lady's-slippers'
or 'Indian moccasins.' They were so different from the familiar
flowers of old Scotland. Several species grew in our meadow
and on shady hillsides – yellow, rose-colored, and some nearly
white, an inch or more in diameter, and shaped exactly like

Indian moccasins. They caught the eye of all the European settlers and made them gaze and wonder like children. And so did calopogon, pogonia, spiranthes, and many other fine plant people that lived in our meadow. The beautiful Turk's-turban (*Lilium superbum*) growing on stream-banks was rare in our neighborhood, but the orange lily grew in abundance on dry ground beneath the bur-oaks and often brought Aunt Ray's lily-bed in Scotland to mind. The butterfly-weed, with its brilliant scarlet flowers, attracted flocks of butterflies and made fine masses of color. With autumn came a glorious abundance and variety of asters, those beautiful plant stars, together with goldenrods, sun-flowers, daisies, and liatris of different species while around the shady margin of the meadow many ferns in beds and vaselike groups spread their beautiful fronds, especially the osmundas (*O. claytoniana*, *regalis*, and *cinnamomea*) and the sensitive and ostrich ferns.

Early in summer we feasted on strawberries, that grew in rich beds beneath the meadow grasses and sedges as well as in the dry sunny woods. And in different bogs and marshes, and around their borders on our own farm and along the Fox River, we found dewberries and cranberries, and a glorious profusion of huckleberries, the fountain-heads of pies of wondrous taste and size, colored in the heart like sunsets. Nor were we slow to discover the value of the hickory trees yielding both sugar and nuts. We carefully counted the different kinds on our farm, and every morning when we could steal a few minutes before breakfast after doing the chores, we visited the trees that had been wounded by the axe, to scrape off and enjoy the thick white delicious syrup that exuded from them, and gathered the nuts as they fell in the mellow Indian summer, making haste to get a fair share with the sapsuckers and squirrels. The hickory makes fine masses of color in the fall, every leaf a flower, but it was the sweet sap and sweet nuts that first interested us. No harvest in the Wisconsin woods was ever gathered with more pleasure and care. Also, to our delight, we found plenty of hazelnuts, and in a few places abundance of wild apples. They were desperately sour, and we used to fill our pockets with them and dare each other to eat one without making a face – no easy feat.

One hot summer day Father told us that we ought to learn to swim. This was one of the most interesting suggestions he had ever offered, but precious little time was allowed for trips to the lake, and he seldom tried to show us how. 'Go to the frogs,' he said, 'and they will give you all the lessons you need. Watch their arms and legs and see how smoothly they kick themselves along and dive and come up. When you want to dive, keep your arms by your side or over your head, and kick, and when you want to come up, let your legs drag and paddle with your hands.'

We found a little basin among the rushes at the south end of the lake, about waist-deep and a rod or two wide, shaped like a sunfish's nest. Here we kicked and plashed for many a lesson, faithfully trying to imitate frogs; but the smooth, comfortable sliding gait of our amphibious teachers seemed hopelessly hard to learn. When we tried to kick frog-fashion, down went our heads as if weighted with lead the moment our feet left the ground. One day it occurred to me to hold my breath as long as I could and let my head sink as far as it liked without paying any attention to it, and try to swim under the water instead of on the surface. This method was a great success, for at the very first trial I managed to cross the basin without touching bottom, and soon learned the use of my limbs. Then, of course, swimming with my head above water soon became so easy that it seemed perfectly natural. David tried the plan with the same success. Then we began to count the number of times that we could swim around the basin without stopping to rest, and after twenty or thirty rounds failed to tire us, we proudly thought that a little more practice would make us about as amphibious as frogs.

On the fourth of July of this swimming year one of the Lawson boys came to visit us, and we went down to the lake to spend the great warm day with the fishes and ducks and turtles. After gliding about on the smooth mirror water, telling stories and enjoying the company of the happy creatures about us, we rowed to our bathing-pool, and David and I went in for a swim, while our companion fished from the boat a little way out beyond the rushes. After a few turns in the pool, it occurred to me that it was now about time to try deep water. Swimming through the thick growth of rushes and lilies was somewhat dangerous, especially for a beginner, because one's arms and legs might be entangled among the long, limber stems; nevertheless I ventured and struck out boldly enough for the boat, where the water was twenty or thirty feet deep. When I reached the end of the little skiff I raised my right hand to take hold of it to surprise Lawson, whose back was toward me and who was not aware of my approach; but I failed to reach high enough, and, of course, the weight of my arm and the stroke against the over-leaning stern of the boat shoved me down and I sank, struggling, frightened and confused. As soon as my feet touched the bottom, I slowly rose to the surface, but before I could get breath enough to call for help, sank back again and lost all control of myself. After sinking and rising I don't know how many times, some water got into my lungs and I began to drown. Then suddenly my mind seemed to clear. I remembered that I could swim under water, and, making a desperate struggle toward the shore, I reached a point where with my toes on the bottom I got my mouth above the surface, gasped for help, and was pulled into the boat.

This humiliating accident spoiled the day, and we all agreed to keep it a profound secret. My sister Sarah had heard my cry for help, and on our arrival at the house inquired what had happened. 'Were you drowning, John? I heard you cry you couldna get oot.' Lawson made haste to reply, 'Oh, no! He was joist haverin'.'

I was very much ashamed of myself, and at night, after calmly reviewing the affair, concluded that there had been no reasonable cause for the accident, and that I ought to punish myself for so nearly losing my life from unmanly fear. Accordingly at the very first opportunity I stole away to the lake by myself, got into my boat, and instead of going back to the old swimming-bowl for further practice, or to try to do sanely and well what I had so ignominiously failed to do in my first adventure, that is, to swim out through the rushes and lilies, I rowed directly out to the middle of the lake, stripped, stood up on the seat in the stern, and with grim deliberation took a header and dove straight down thirty or forty feet, turned easily, and, letting my feet drag, paddled straight to the surface with my hands as Father had at first directed me to do. I then swam round the boat, glorying in my suddenly acquired confidence and victory over myself, climbed into it, and dived again, with the same triumphant success. I think I went down four or five times, and each time as I made the dive-spring shouted aloud, 'Take that!' feeling that was getting most gloriously even with myself.

Never again from that day to this have I lost control of myself in water. If suddenly thrown overboard at sea in the dark, or even while asleep, I think I would immediately right myself in a way some would call 'instinct,' rise among the waves, catch my breath, and try to plan what would better be done. Never was victory over self more complete. I have been a good swimmer ever since. At a slow gait I think I could swim all day in smooth water moderate in temperature. When I was a student at Madison, I used to go on long swimming-journeys, called exploring expeditions, along the south shore of Lake Mendota, on Saturdays, sometimes alone, sometimes with another amphibious explorer by the name of Fuller.

My adventures in Fountain Lake call to mind the story of a boy who in climbing a tree to rob a crow's nest fell and broke his leg, but as soon as it healed compelled himself to climb to the top of the tree he had fallen from.

Like Scotch children in general we were taught grim self-denial, in season and out of season, to mortify the flesh, keep our bodies in subjection to Bible laws, and mercilessly punish ourselves for every fault imagined or committed. A little boy, while helping his sister to drive home the cows, happened to use a forbidden word. 'I'll have to tell Fayther on ye,' said the horrified sister. 'I'll tell him that ye said a bad word.' 'Weel,' said the boy, by way of excuse, 'I couldna help the word comin' into me, and it's na waur to speak it oot than to let it rin through ye.'

A Scotch fiddler playing at a wedding drank so much whiskey that on the way home he fell by the roadside. In the morning he was ashamed and angry and determined to punish himself. Making haste to the house of a friend, a gamekeeper, he called him out, and requested the loan of a gun. The alarmed gamekeeper, not liking the fiddler's looks and voice, anxiously inquired what he was going to do with it. 'Surely,' said he, 'you're no gan to shoot yourself.' 'No-o,' with characteristic candor replied the penitent fiddler, 'I dinna think that I'll juist exactly kill mysel,.but I'm gaun to tak a dander doon the burn (brook) wi' the gull and gie mysel a deevil o' a fleg (fright)'.

One calm summer evening a red-headed woodpecker was drowned in our lake. The accident happened at the south end, opposite our memorable swimming-hole, a few rods from the place where I came so near being drowned years before. I had returned to the old home during a summer vacation of the State University, and, having made a beginning in botany, I was, of course, full of enthusiasm and ran eagerly to my beloved pogonia, calopogon, and cypripedium gardens, osmunda ferneries, and the lake lilies and pitcher-plants. A little before sundown the day-breeze died away, and the lake, reflecting the wooded hills like a mirror, was dimpled and dotted and streaked here and there where fishes and turtles were poking out their heads and muskrats were sculling themselves along with their flat tails making glittering tracks. After lingering awhile, dreamily recalling the old, hard, half-happy days, and watching my favorite red-headed woodpeckers pursuing moths like regular flycatchers, I swam out through the rushes and up the middle of the lake to the north end and back, gliding slowly, looking about me, enjoying the scenery as I would in a saunter along the shore, and studying the habits of the animals as they were explained and recorded on the smooth glassy water.

On the way back, when I was within a hundred rods or so of

the end of my voyage, I noticed a peculiar plashing disturbance that could not, I thought, be made by a jumping fish or any other inhabitant of the lake; for instead of low regular out-circling ripples such as are made by the popping up of a head or like those raised by the quick splash of a leaping fish, or diving loon or muskrat, a continuous struggle was kept up for several minutes ere the outspreading, interfering ring-waves began to die away. Swimming hastily to the spot to try to discover what had happened, I found one of my woodpeckers floating motionless with outspread wings. All was over. Had I been a minute or two earlier, I might have saved him. He had glanced on the water I suppose in pursuit of a moth, was unable to rise from it, and died struggling, as I nearly did at this same spot. Like me he seemed to have lost his mind in blind confusion and fear. The water was warm, and had he kept still with his head a little above the surface, he would sooner or later have been wafted ashore. The best aimed flights of birds and man 'gang aft agley,' but this was the first case I had witnessed of a bird losing its life by drowning.

Doubtless accidents to animals are far more common than is generally known. I have seen quails killed by flying against our house when suddenly startled. Some birds get entangled in hairs of their own nests and die. Once I found a poor snipe in our meadow that was unable to fly on account of difficult egg-birth. Pitying the poor mother, I picked her up out of the grass and helped her as gently as I could, and as soon as the egg was born she flew gladly away. Oftentimes I have thought it strange that one could walk through the woods and mountains and plains for years without seeing a single blood-spot. Most wild animals get into the world and out of it without being noticed. Nevertheless we at last sadly learn that they are all subject to the vicissitudes of fortune like ourselves. Many birds lose their lives in storms. I remember a particularly severe Wisconsin winter, when the temperature was many degrees below zero and the snow was deep, preventing the quail, which feed on the ground, from getting anything like enough of food, as was pitifully shown by a flock I found on our farm frozen solid in a thicket of oak sprouts. They were in a circle about a foot wide, with their heads outward, packed close together for warmth. Yet all had died without a struggle, perhaps more from starvation than frost. Many small birds lose their lives in the storms of early spring, or even summer. One mild spring morning I picked up more than a score out of the grass and flowers, most of them darling singers that had perished in a sudden storm of sleety rain and hail.

In a hollow at the foot of an oak tree that I had chopped down one cold winter day, I found a poor ground squirrel frozen solid in its snug grassy nest, in the middle of a store of nearly a peck of wheat it had carefully gathered. I carried it home and gradually thawed and warmed it in the kitchen, hoping it would come to life like a pickerel I caught in our lake through a hole in the ice, which, after being frozen as hard as a bone and thawed at the fireside, squirmed itself out of the grasp of the cook when she began to scrape it, bounced off the table, and danced about on the floors making wonderful springy jumps as if trying to find its way back home to the lake. But for the poor spermophile nothing I could do in the way of revival was of any avail. Its life had passed away without the slightest struggle, as it lay asleep curled up like a ball, with its tail wrapped about it.

Chapter 4

A PARADISE OF BIRDS

The Wisconsin oak openings were a summer paradise for song birds, and a fine place to get acquainted with them; for the trees stood wide apart, allowing one to see the happy home-seekers as they arrived in the spring, their mating, nest-building, the brooding and feeding of the young, and, after they were full-fledged and strong, to see all the families of the neighborhood gathering and getting ready to leave in the fall. Excepting the geese and ducks and pigeons nearly all our summer birds arrived singly or in small draggled flocks, but when frost and falling leaves brought their winter homes to mind they assembled in large flocks on dead or leafless trees by the side of a meadow or field, perhaps to get acquainted and talk the thing over. Some species held regular daily meetings for several weeks before finally setting forth on their long southern journeys. Strange to say, we never saw them start. Some mornings we would find them gone. Doubtless they migrated in the night time. Comparatively few species remained all winter, the nuthatch, chickadee, owl, prairie chicken, quail, and a few stragglers from the main flocks of ducks, jays, hawks, and bluebirds. Only after the country was settled did either jays or bluebirds winter with us.

The brave, frost-defying chickadees and nuthatches stayed all the year wholly independent of farms and man's food and affairs.

With the first hints of spring came the brave little bluebirds, darling singers as blue as the best sky, and of course we all loved them. Their rich, crispy warbling is perfectly delightful, soothing and cheering, sweet and whisperingly low, Nature's fine love touches, every note going straight home into one's heart. And withal they are hardy and brave, fearless fighters in defense of home. When we boys approached their knot-hole nests, the bold little fellows kept scolding and diving at us and tried to strike us in the face, and oftentimes we were afraid they would prick our eyes. But the boldness of the little house-keepers only made us love them the more.

None of the bird people of Wisconsin welcomed us more heartily than the common robin. Far from showing alarm at the coming of settlers into their native woods, they reared their young around our gardens as if they liked us, and how heartily we admired the beauty and fine manners of these graceful birds and their loud cheery song of *Fear not, fear not, cheer up, cheer up*. It was easy to love them for they reminded us of the robin redbreast of Scotland. Like the bluebirds, they dared every danger in defense of home, and we often wondered that birds so gentle could be so bold and that sweet-voiced singers could so fiercely fight and scold.

Of all the great singers that sweeten Wisconsin one of the best known and best loved is the brown thrush or thrasher, strong and able without being familiar, and easily seen and heard. Rosy purple evenings after thunder-showers are the favorite song-times, when the winds have died away and the steaming ground and the leaves and flowers fill the air with fragrance. Then the male makes haste to the topmost spray of an oak tree and sings loud and clear with delightful enthusiasm until sundown, mostly I suppose for his mate sitting on the precious eggs in a brush heap. And how faithful and watchful and daring he is! Woe to the snake or squirrel that ventured to go nigh the nest! We often saw him diving on them, pecking them about the head and driving them away as bravely as the kingbird drives away hawks. Their rich and varied strains make the air fairly quiver. We boys often tried to interpret the wild ringing melody and put it into words.

After the arrival of the thrushes came the bobolinks, gushing, gurgling, inexhaustible fountains of song, pouring forth floods of sweet notes over the broad Fox River meadows in wonderful variety and volume, crowded and miffed beyond description, as they hovered on quivering wings above their hidden nests in the grass. It seemed marvelous to us that birds so moderate in size could hold so much of this wonderful song stuff. Each one of them poured forth music enough for a whole flock, singing as if its whole body, feathers and all, were made up of music, flowing, glowing, bubbling melody interpenetrated here and there with small scintillating prickles and spicules. We never became so intimately acquainted with the bobolinks as with the thrushes, for they lived far out on the broad Fox River meadows, while the thrushes sang on the tree-tops around every home. The bobolinks were among the first of our great singers to leave us in the fall, going apparently direct to the rice-fields of the Southern States, where they grew fat and were slaughtered in countless numbers for food. Sad fate for singers so purely divine.

One of the gayest of the singers is the redwing blackbird. In the spring, when his scarlet epaulets shine brightest, and his little modest gray wife is sitting on the nest, built on rushes in a swamp, he sits on a near-by oak and devotedly sings almost all day. His rich simple strain is *baumpalee*, *baumpalee*, or *bobalee* as interpreted by some. In summer, after nesting cares are over, they assemble in flocks of hundreds and thousands to feast on Indian corn when it is in the milk. Scattering over a field, each selects an ear, strips the husk down far enough to lay bare an inch or two of the end of it, enjoys an exhilarating feast, and after all are full they rise simultaneously with a quick birr of wings like an old-fashioned church congregation fluttering to their feet when the minister after giving out the hymn says, 'Let the congregation arise and sing.' Alighting on near-by trees, they sing with a hearty vengeance, bursting out without any puttering prelude in gloriously glad concert, hundreds or thousands of exulting voices with sweet gurgling *baumpalees* mingled with chippy vibrant and exploding globules of musical notes, making a most enthusiastic, indescribable joy-song, a combination unlike anything to be heard elsewhere in the bird kingdom; something like bagpipes, flutes, violins, pianos, and human-like voices all bursting and bubbling at once. Then suddenly someone of the joyful congregation shouts Chirr! Chirr! and all stop as if shot.

The sweet-voiced meadowlark with its placid, simple song of *peery-eery-odical* was another favorite, and we soon learned to admire the Baltimore oriole and its wonderful hanging nests, and the scarlet tanager glowing like fire amid the green leaves.

But no singer of them all got farther into our hearts than the little speckle-breasted song sparrow, one of the first to arrive and begin nest-building and singing. The richness, sweetness, and pathos of this small darling's song as he sat on a low bush often brought tears to our eyes.

The little cheery, modest chickadee midget, loved by every innocent boy and girl, man and woman, and by many not altogether innocent, was one of the first of the birds to attract our attention, drawing nearer and nearer to us as the winter advanced, bravely singing his faint silvery, lisping, tinkling notes ending with a bright *dee, dee, dee!* however frosty the weather.

The nuthatches, who also stayed all winter with us, were favorites with us boys. We loved to watch them as they traced the bark-furrows of the oaks and hickories head downward, deftly flicking off loose scales and splinters in search of insects, and braving the coldest weather as if their little sparks of life were as safely warm in winter as in summer, unquenchable by the severest frost. With the help of the chickadees they made a delightful stir in the solemn winter days, and when we were out chopping we never ceased to wonder how their slender flaked toes could be kept warm when our own were so painfully frosted though clad in thick socks and boots. And we wondered and admired the more when we thought of the little midgets sleeping in knot-holes when the temperature was far below zero, sometimes thirty-five degrees below, and in the morning, after a minute breakfast of a few frozen insects and hoarfrost crystals, playing and chatting in cheery tones as if food, weather, and everything was according to their own warm hearts. Our Yankee told us that the name of this darling was Devil-downhead.

Their big neighbors the owls also made good winter music, singing out loud in wild, gallant strains bespeaking brave comfort, let the frost bite as it might. The solemn hooting of the species with the widest throat seemed to us the very wildest of all the winter sounds.

Prairie chickens crane strolling in family flocks about the shanty, picking seeds and grasshoppers like domestic fowls, and they became still more abundant as wheat-and-corn-fields were multiplied, but also wilder, of course, when every shotgun in the country was aimed at them. The booming of the males during the mating-season was one of the loudest and strangest of the early spring sounds being easily heard on calm mornings at a distance of a half or three fourths of a mile. As soon as the snow was off the ground, they assembled in flocks of a dozen or two on an open spot, usually on the side of a ploughed field, ruffled up their feathers, inflated the curious colored sacks on the sides of their necks, and strutted about with queer gestures something like turkey gobblers, uttering strange loud, rounded, drumming calls – *boom! boom! boom!* interrupted by choking sounds. My brother Daniel caught one while she was sitting on her nest in our corn-field. The young are just like domestic chicks, run with the mother as soon as hatched, and stay with her until autumn, feeding on the ground, never taking wing unless disturbed. In winter, when full-grown, they assemble in large flocks, fly about sundown to selected roosting-places on tall trees, and to feeding-places in the morning – unhusked corn-fields, if any are to be found in the neighborhood, or thickets of dwarf birch and willows, the buds of which furnish a considerable part of their food when snow covers the ground.

The wild rice-marshes along the Fox River and around Pucaway Lake were the summer homes of millions of ducks, and in the Indian summer, when the rice was ripe, they grew very fat. The magnificent mallards in particular afforded our Yankee neighbors royal feasts almost without price, for often as many as a half-dozen were killed at a shot, but we seldom were allowed a single hour for hunting and so got very few. The autumn duck season was a glad time for the Indians also, for they feasted and grew fat not only on the ducks but on the wild rice, large quantities of which they gathered as they glided through the midst of the generous crop in canoes, bending down handfuls over the sides, and beating out the grain with small paddles.

The warmth of the deep spring fountains of the creek in our meadow kept it open all the year, and a few pairs of wood ducks, the most beautiful, we thought, of all the ducks, wintered in it. I well remember the first specimen I ever saw. Father shot it in the creek during a snowstorm, brought it into the house, and called us around him, saying: 'Come, bairns, and admire the work of God displayed in this bonnie bird. Naebody but God could paint feathers like these. Juist look at the colors, hoo they shine, and hoo fine they overlap and blend thegether like the colors o' the rainbow.' And we all agreed that never, never before had we seen so awfu' bonnie a bird. A pair nested every year in the hollow top of an oak stump about fifteen feet high that stood on the side of the meadow, and we used to wonder how they got the fluffy young ones down from the nest and across the meadow to the lake when they were only helpless, featherless midgets; whether the mother carried them to the water on her back or in her mouth. I never saw the thing done or found anybody who had until this summer, when Mr Holabird, a keen observer, told me that he once saw the mother carry them from the nest tree in her mouth, quickly coming and going to a near-by stream, and in a few minutes get them all together and proudly sail away.

Sometimes a flock of swans was seen passing over at a great height on their long journeys, and we admired their clear bugle notes, but they seldom visited any of the lakes in our neighborhood, so seldom that when they did it was talked of for years. One was shot by a blacksmith on a millpond with a long-range Sharp's rifle, and many of the neighbors went far to see it.

The common gray goose, Canada honker, flying in regular harrow-shaped flocks, was one of the wildest and wariest of all the large birds that enlivened the spring and autumn. They seldom ventured to alight in our small lake, fearing, I suppose, that hunters might be concealed in the rushes; but on account of their fondness for the young leaves of winter wheat when they were a few inches high, they often alighted on our fields when passing on their way south, and occasionally even in our corn-fields when a snowstorm was blowing and they were hungry and wing-weary, with nearly an inch of snow on their backs. In such times of distress we used to pity them, even while trying to get a shot at them. They were exceedingly cautious and cir-cumspect; usually flew several times round the adjacent thickets and fences to make sure that no enemy was near before settling down, and one always stood on guard, relieved from time to time, while the flock was feeding. Therefore there was no chance to creep up on them unobserved; you had to be well hidden before the flock arrived. It was the ambition of boys to be able to shoot these wary birds. I never got but two, both of them at one so-called lucky shot. When I ran to pick them up, one of them flew away, but as the poor fellow was sorely wounded he didn't fly far. When I caught him after a short chase, he uttered a piercing cry of terror and despair, which the leader of the flock heard at a distance of about a hundred rods. They had flown off in frightened disorder, of course, but had got into the regular harrow-shape order when the leader heard the cry, and I shall never forget how bravely he left his place at the head of the flock and hurried back screaming and struck at me in trying to save his companion. I dodged down and held my hands over my head, and thus escaped a blow of his elbows. Fortunately I had left my gun at the fence, and the life of this noble bird was spared after he had risked it in trying to save his wounded friend or neighbor or family relation. For so shy a bird boldly to attack a hunter showed wonderful sympathy and courage. This is one of my strangest hunting experiences. Never before had I regarded wild geese as dangerous, or capable of such noble, self-sacrificing devotion.

The loud, clear call of the handsome bob-whites was one of the pleasantest and most characteristic of our spring sounds, and we soon learned to imitate it so well that a bold cock often accepted our challenge and came flying to fight. The young run as soon as they are hatched and follow their parents until spring, roosting on the ground in a close bunch, heads out ready to scatter and fly. These fine birds were seldom seen when we first arrived in the wilderness, but when wheat-fields supplied abundance of food they multiplied very fast, although oftentimes sore pressed during hard winters when the snow reached a depth of two or three feet, covering their food, while the mercury fell to twenty or thirty degrees below zero. Occasionally, although shy on account of being persistently hunted, under pressure of extreme hunger in the very coldest weather when the snow was deepest they ventured into barn-yards and even approached the doorsteps of houses, searching for any sort of scraps and crumbs, as if piteously begging for food. One of our neighbors saw a flock come creeping up through the snow, unable to fly, hardly able to walk, and while approaching the door several of them actually fell down and died; showing that birds, usually so vigorous and apparently independent of fortune, suffer and lose their lives in extreme weather like the rest of us, frozen to death like settlers caught in blizzards. None of our neighbors perished in storms, though many had feet, ears, and fingers frost-nipped or solidly frozen.

As soon as the lake ice melted, we heard the lonely cry of the loon, one of the wildest and most striking of all the wilderness sounds, a strange, sad, mournful, unearthly cry, half laughing, half wailing. Nevertheless the great northern diver, as our species is called, is a brave, hardy, beautiful bird, able to fly under water about as well as above it, and to spear and capture the swiftest fishes for food. Those that haunted our lake were so wary none was shot for years, though every boy hunter in the neighborhood was ambitious to get one to prove his skill. On one of our bitter cold New Year holidays I was surprised to see a loon in the small open part of the lake at the mouth of the inlet that was kept from freezing by the warm spring water. I knew that it could not fly out of so small a place, for these heavy birds have to beat the water for half a mile or so before they can get fairly on the wing. Their narrow, finlike wings are very small as compared with the weight of the body and are evidently made for flying through water as well as through the air, and it is by means of their swift flight through the water and the swiftness of the blow they strike with their long, spear-like bills that they are able to capture the fishes on which they feed. I ran down the meadow with the gun, got into my boat, and pursued that poor winter-bound straggler. Of course he dived again and again, but had to come up to breathe, and I at length got a quick shot at his head and slightly wounded or stunned him, caught him, and ran proudly back to the house with my prize. I carried him in my arms; he didn't struggle to get away or offer to strike me, and when I put him on the floor in front of the kitchen stove, he just rested quietly on his belly as noiseless and motionless as if he were a stuffed specimen on a shelf, held his neck erect, gave no sign of suffering from any wound, and though he was motionless, his small black eyes seemed to be ever keenly watchful. His formidable bill, very sharp, three or three and a half inches long, and shaped like a pickaxe, was held perfectly level. But the wonder was that he did not struggle or make the slightest movement. We had a tortoiseshell cat, an old Tom of great experience, who was so fond of lying under the stove in frosty weather that it was difficult even to poke him out with a broom; but when he saw and smelled that strange big fishy, black and white, speckledy bird, the like of which he had never before seen, he rushed wildly to the farther corner of the kitchen, looked back cautiously and suspiciously, and began to make a careful study of the handsome but dangerous looking stranger. Becoming more and more curious and interested, he at length advanced a step or two for a nearer new and nearer smell; and as the wonderful bird kept absolutely motionless, he was encouraged to venture gradually nearer and nearer until within perhaps five or six feet of its breast. Then the wary loon, not liking Tom's looks in so near a view, which perhaps recalled to his mind the plundering minks and muskrats he had to fight when they approached his nest, prepared to defend himself by slowly, almost imperceptibly drawing back his long pickaxe bill, and without the slightest fuss or stir held it level and ready just over his tail. With that dangerous bill drawn so far back out of the way, Tom's confidence in the stranger's peaceful intentions seemed almost complete, and, thus encouraged, he at last ventured forward with wondering, questioning eyes and quivering nostrils until he was only eighteen or twenty inches from the loon's smooth white breast. When the beautiful bird, apparently as peaceful and inoffensive as a flower, saw that his hairy yellow enemy had arrived at the right distance, the loon, who evidently was a fine judge of the reach of his spear, shot it forward quick as a lightning-flash, in marvelous contrast to the wonderful slowness of the preparatory poising, backward motion. The aim was true to a hairbreadth. Tom was struck right in the centre of his forehead, between the eyes. I thought his skull was cracked. Perhaps it was. The sudden astonishment of that outraged cat, the virtuous indignation and wrath, terror, and pain, are far beyond description. His eyes and screams and desperate retreat told all that. When the blow was received, he made a noise that I never heard a cat make before or since; an awfully deep, condensed, screechy, explosive *Wuck!* as he bounced straight up in the air like a bucking bronco; and when he alighted after his spring, he rushed madly across the room and made frantic efforts to climb up the hard-finished plaster wall. Not satisfied to get the width of the kitchen away from his mysterious enemy, for the first time that cold winter he tried to get out of the house, anyhow, anywhere out of that loon-infested room. When he finally ventured to look back and saw that the barbarous bird was still there, tranquil and motionless in front of the stove, he regained command of some of his shattered senses and carefully commenced to examine his wound. Backed against the wall in the farthest corner, and keeping his eye on the outrageous bird, he tenderly touched and washed the sore spot, wetting his paw with his tongue, pausing now and then as his courage increased to glare and stare and growl at his enemy with looks and tones wonderfully human, as if saying: 'You confounded fishy, unfair rascal! What did you do that for? What had I done to you? Faithless, legless, long-nosed wretch!' Intense experiences like the above bring out the humanity that is in all animals. One touch of nature, even a cat-and-loon touch, makes all the world kin.

It was a great memorable day when the first flock of passenger pigeons came to our farm, calling to mind the story we had read about them when we were at school in Scotland. Of all God's feathered people that sailed the Wisconsin sky, no other bird seemed to us so wonderful. The beautiful wanderers flew like the winds in flocks of millions from climate to climate in accord with the weather, finding their food – acorns, beechnuts, pine-nuts, cranberries, strawberries, huckleberries, juniper berries, hackberries, buckwheat, rice, wheat, oats, corn – in fields and forests thousands of miles apart. I have seen flocks streaming south in the fall so large that they were flowing over from horizon to horizon in an almost continuous stream all day long, at the rate of forty or fifty miles an hour, like a mighty river in the sky, widening, contracting, descending like falls and cataracts, and rising suddenly here and there in huge ragged masses like high-plashing spray. How wonderful the distances they flew in a day – in a year – in a lifetime! They arrived in Wisconsin in the spring just after the sun had cleared away the snow, and alighted in the woods to feed on the fallen acorns that they had missed the previous autumn. A comparatively small flock swept thousands of acres perfectly clean of acorns in a few minutes, by moving straight ahead with a broad front. All got their share, for the rear constantly became the van by flying over the flock and alighting in front, the entire flock constantly changing from rear to front, revolving something like a wheel with a low buzzing wing roar that could be heard a long way off. In summer they feasted on wheat and oats and were easily approached as they rested on the trees along the sides of the field after a good full meal, displaying beautiful iridescent colors as they moved their necks backward and forward when we went very near them. Every shotgun was aimed at them and everybody feasted on pigeon pies, and not a few of the settlers feasted also on the beauty of the wonderful birds. The breast of the male is a fine rosy red, the lower part of the neck behind and along the sides changing from the red of the breast to gold, emerald green and rich crimson. The general color of the upper parts is grayish blue, the under parts white. The extreme length of the bird is about seventeen inches; the finely modeled slender tail about eight inches, and extent of wings twenty-four inches. The females are scarcely less beautiful. 'Oh, what bonnie, bonnie birds!' we exclaimed over the first that fell into our hands. 'Oh, what colors! Look at their breasts, bonnie as roses, and at their necks aglow wi' every color juist like the wonderfu' wood ducks. Oh, the bonnie, bonnie creatures, they beat a'! Where did they a' come fra, and where are they a' gan? It's awfu' like a sin to kill them!' To this some smug, practical old sinner would remark: 'Aye, it's a peety, as ye say, to kill the bonnie things, but they were made to be killed, and sent for us to eat as the quails were sent to God's chosen people, the Israelites, when they were starving in the desert ayont the Red Sea. And I must confess that meat was never put up in neater, handsomer-painted packages.'

In the New England and Canada woods beechnuts were their best and most abundant food, farther north, cranberries and huckleberries. After everything was cleaned up in the north and winter was coming on, they went south for rice, corn, acorns, haws, wild grapes, crab-apples, sparkle-berries, etc. They seemed to require more than half of the continent for feeding-grounds, moving from one table to another, field to field, forest to forest, finding something ripe and wholesome all the year round. In going south in the fine Indian-summer weather they flew high and followed one another, though the head of the flock might be hundreds of miles in advance. But against head winds they took advantage of the inequalities of the ground, flying comparatively low. All followed the leader's ups and downs over hill and dale though far out of sight, never hesitating at any turn of the way, vertical or horizontal that the leaders had taken, though the largest flocks stretched across several States, and belts of different kinds of weather.

There were no roosting- or breeding-places near our farm, and I never saw any of them until long after the great flocks were exterminated. I therefore quote, from Audubon's and Pokagon's vivid descriptions.

'Toward evening,' Audubon says, 'they depart for the roosting-place, which may be hundreds of miles distant. One on the banks of Green River, Kentucky, was over three miles wide and forty long.'

'My first view of it,' says the great naturalist, 'was about a fortnight after it had been chosen by the birds, and I arrived there nearly two hours before sunset. Few pigeons were then to be seen, but a great many persons with horses and wagons and armed with guns, long poles, sulphur pots, pine pitch torches, etc., had already established encampments on the borders. Two farmers had driven upwards of three hundred hogs a distance of more than a hundred miles to be fattened on slaughtered pigeons. Here and there the people employed in plucking and salting what had already been secured were sitting in the midst of piles of birds. Dung several inches thick covered the ground. Many trees two feet in diameter were broken off at no great distance from the ground, and the branches of many of the tallest and largest had given way, as if the forest had been swept by a tornado.

'Not a pigeon had arrived at sundown. Suddenly a general cry arose – ' Here they come!' The noise they made, though still distant, reminded me of a hard gale at sea passing through the rigging of a close-reefed ship. Thousands were soon knocked down by the pole-men. The birds continued to pour in. The fires were lighted and a magnificent as well as terrifying sight presented itself. The pigeons pouring in alighted everywhere, one above another, until solid masses were formed on the branches all around. Here and there the perches gave way with a crash, and falling destroyed hundreds beneath, forcing down the dense groups with which every stick was loaded; a scene of uproar and conflict. I found it useless to speak or even to shout to those persons nearest me. Even the reports of the guns were seldom heard, and I was made aware of the firing only by seeing the shooters reloading. None dared venture within the line of devastation. The hogs had been penned up in due time, the picking up of the dead and wounded being left for the next morning's employment. The pigeons were constantly coming in and it was after midnight before I perceived a decrease in the number of those that arrived. The uproar continued all night, and, anxious to know how far the sound reached I sent off a man who, returning two hours after, informed me that he had heard it distinctly three miles distant.

'Toward daylight the noise in some measure subsided; long before objects were distinguishable the pigeons began to move off in a direction quite different from that in which they had arrived the evening before, and at sunrise all that were able to fly had disappeared. The howling of the wolves now reached our ears, and the foxes, lynxes, cougars, bears, coons, opossums, and polecats were seen sneaking off, while eagles and hawks of different species, accompanied by a crowd of vultures, came to supplant them and enjoy a share of the spoil.

'Then the authors of all this devastation began their entry amongst the dead, the dying and mangled. The pigeons were picked up and piled in heaps until each had as many as they could possibly dispose of, when the hogs were let loose to feed on the remainder.

'The breeding-places are selected with reference to abundance of food, and countless myriads resort to them. At this period the note of the pigeon is *coo coo coo*, like that of the domestic species but much shorter. They caress by billing, and during incubation the male supplies the female with food. As the young grow, the tyrant of creation appears to disturb the peaceful scene, armed with axes to chop down the squab-laden trees, and the abomination of desolation and destruction produced far surpasses even that of the roosting places.'

Pokagon, an educated Indian writer, says: 'I saw one nesting-place in Wisconsin one hundred miles long and from three to ten miles wide. Every tree, some of them quite low and scrubby, had from one to fifty nests on each. Some of the nests overflow from the oaks to the hemlock and pine woods. When the pigeon hunters attack the breeding-places they sometimes cut the timber from thousands of acres. Millions are caught in nets with salt or grain for bait, and schooners, sometimes loaded down with the birds, are taken to New York, where they are sold for a cent apiece.'

Chapter 5

YOUNG HUNTERS

In the older eastern States it used to be considered great sport for an army of boys to assemble to hunt birds, squirrels, and every other unclaimed, unprotected live thing of shootable size. They divided into two squads, and, choosing leaders, scattered through the woods in different directions, and the party that killed the greatest number enjoyed a supper at the expense of the other. The whole neighborhood seemed to enjoy the shameful sport, especially the farmers afraid of their crops. With a great air of importance, laws were enacted to govern the gory business. For example, a gray squirrel must count four heads, a woodchuck six heads, common red squirrel two heads, black squirrel ten heads, a partridge five heads, the larger birds, such as whip-poor-wills and nighthawks two heads each, the wary crows three, and bob-whites three. But all the blessed company of mere songbirds, warblers, robins, thrushes, orioles, with nuthatches, chickadees, blue jays, woodpeckers, etc., counted only one head each. The heads of the birds were hastily wrung off and thrust into the game-bags to be counted, saving the bodies only of what were called game, the larger squirrels, bob-whites, partridges, etc. The blood-stained bags of the best slayers were soon bulging full. Then at a given hour all had to stop and repair to the town, empty their dripping sacks, count the heads, and go rejoicing to their dinner. Although, like other wild boys, I was fond of shooting, I never had anything to do with these abominable head-hunts. And now the farmers having learned that birds are their friends wholesale slaughter has been abolished.

We seldom saw deer, though their tracks were common. The Yankee explained that they traveled and fed mostly at night, and hid in tamarack swamps and brushy places in the daytime, and how the Indians knew all about them and could find them whenever they were hungry.

Indians belonging to the Menominee and Winnebago occasionally visited us at our cabin to get a piece of bread or some matches, or to sharpen their knives on our grindstone, and we boys watched them closely to see that they didn't steal Jack. We wondered at their knowledge of animals when we saw them go direct to trees on our farm, chop holes in them with their tomahawks and take out coons, of the existence of which we had never noticed the slightest trace. In winter, after the first snow, we frequently saw three or four Indians hunting deer in company, running like hounds on the fresh, exciting tracks. The escape of the deer from these noiseless, tireless hunters was said to be well-nigh impossible; they were followed to the death.

Most of our neighbors brought some sort of gun from the old country, but seldom took time to hunt, even after the first hard work of fencing and clearing was over, except to shoot a duck or prairie chicken now and then that happened to come in their way. It was only the less industrious American settlers who left their work to go far a-hunting. Two or three of our most enterprising American neighbors went off every fall with their teams to the pine regions and cranberry marshes in the northern part of the State to hunt and gather berries. I well remember seeing their wagons loaded with game when they returned from a successful hunt. Their loads consisted usually of half a dozen deer or more, one or two black bears, and fifteen or twenty bushels of cranberries; all solidly frozen. Part of both the berries and meat was usually sold in Portage; the balance furnished their families with abundance of venison, bear grease, and pies.

Winter wheat is sown in the fall, and when it is a month or so old the deer, like the wild geese, are very fond of it, especially since other kinds of food are then becoming scarce. One of our neighbors across the Fox River killed a large number, some thirty or forty, on a small patch of wheat, simply by lying in wait for them every night. Our wheat-field was the first that was sown in the neighborhood. The deer soon found it and came in every night to feast, but it was eight or nine years before we ever disturbed them. David then killed one deer, the only one killed by any of our family. He went out shortly after sundown at the time of full moon to one of our wheat-fields, carrying a double-barreled shotgun loaded with buck-shot. After lying in wait an hour or so, he saw a doe and her fawn jump the fence and come cautiously into the wheat. After they were within sixty or seventy yards of him, he was surprised when he tried to take aim that about half of the moon's disc was mysteriously darkened as if covered by the edge of a dense cloud. This proved to be an eclipse. Nevertheless, he fired at the mother, and she immediately ran off, jumped the fence, and took to the woods by the way she came. The fawn danced about bewildered, wondering what had become of its mother, but finally fled to the woods. David fired at the poor deserted thing as it ran past him but happily missed it. Hearing the shots, I joined David to learn his luck. He said he thought he must have wounded the mother, and when we were strolling about in the woods in search of her we saw three or four deer on their way to the wheat-field, led by a fine buck. They were walking rapidly, but cautiously halted at intervals of a few rods to listen and look ahead and scent the air. They failed to notice us, though by this time the moon was out of the eclipse shadow and we were standing only about fifty yards from them. I was carrying the gun. David had fired both barrels but when he was reloading one of them he happened to put the wad intended to cover the shot into the empty barrel, and so when we were climbing over the fence the buckshot had rolled out, and when I fired at the big buck I knew by the report that there was nothing but powder in the charge. The startled deer danced about in confusion for a few seconds, uncertain which way to run until they caught sight of us, when they bounded off through the woods. Next morning we found the poor mother lying about three hundred yards from the place where she was shot. She had run this distance and jumped a high fence after one of the buckshot had passed through her heart.

Excepting Sundays we boys had only two days of the year to ourselves, the 4th of July and the 1st of January. Sundays were less than half our own, on account of Bible lessons, Sunday-school lessons and church services; all the others were labour days, rain or shine, cold or warm. No wonder, then, that our two holidays were precious and that it was not easy to decide what to do with them. They were usually spent on the highest rocky hill in the neighborhood, called the Observatory; in visiting our boy friends on adjacent farms to hunt, fish, wrestle, and play games; in reading some new favorite book we had managed to borrow or buy; or in making models of machines I had invented.

One of our July days was spent with two Scotch boys of our own age hunting redwing blackbirds then busy in the corn-fields. Our party had only one single-barreled shotgun, which, as the oldest and perhaps because I was thought to be the best shot, I had the honor of carrying. We marched through the corn without getting sight of a single redwing, but just as we reached the far side of the field, a red-headed woodpecker flew up, and the Lawson boys cried: 'Shoot him! Shoot him! he is just as bad as a blackbird. He eats corn!' This memorable woodpecker alighted in the top of a white oak tree about fifty feet high. I fired from a position almost immediately beneath him, and he fell straight down at my feet. When I picked him up and was admiring his plumage, he moved his legs slightly, and I said, 'Poor bird, he's no deed yet and we'll hae to kill him to put him oot o' pain,' – sincerely pitying him, after we had taken pleasure in shooting him. I had seen servant girls wringing chicken necks, so with desperate humanity I took the limp unfortunate by the head, swung him around three or four times thinking I was wringing his neck, and then threw him hard on the ground to quench the last possible spark of life and make quick death doubly sure. But to our astonishment the moment he struck the ground he gave a cry of alarm and flew right straight up like a rejoicing lark into the top of the same tree, and perhaps to the same branch he had fallen from, and began to adjust his ruffled feathers, nodding and chirping and looking down at us as if wondering what in the bird world we had been doing to him. This of course banished all thought of killing, as far as that revived woodpecker was concerned, no matter how many ears of corn he might spoil, and we all heartily congratulated him on his wonderful, triumphant resurrection from three kinds of death – shooting, neck-wringing, and destructive concussion. I suppose only one pellet had touched him, glancing on his head.

Another extraordinary shooting-affair happened one summer morning shortly after daybreak. When I went to the stable to feed the horses I noticed a big white-breasted hawk on a tall oak in front of the chicken-house, evidently waiting for a chicken breakfast. I ran to the house for the gun, and when I fired he fell about halfway down the tree, caught a branch with his claws, hung back downward and fluttered a few seconds, then managed to stand erect. I fired again to put him out of pain, and to my surprise the second shot seemed to restore his strength instead of killing him, for he flew out of the tree and over the meadow with strong and regular wing-beats for thirty or forty rods apparently as well as ever, but died suddenly in the air and dropped like a stone.

We hunted muskrats whenever we had time to run down to the lake. They are brown bunchy animals about twenty-three inches long, the tail being about nine inches in length, black in color and flattened vertically for sculling, and the hind feet are half-webbed. They look like little beavers, usually have from ten to a dozen young, are easily tamed and make interesting pets. We liked to watch them at their work and at their meals. In the spring when the snow vanishes and the lake ice begins to melt, the first open spot is always used as a feeding-place, where they dive from the edge of the ice and in a minute or less reappear with a mussel or a mouthful of pontederia or water-lily leaves, climb back on to the ice and sit up to nibble their food, handling it very much like squirrels or marmots. It is then that they are most easily shot, a solitary hunter oftentimes shooting thirty or forty in a single day. Their nests on the rushy margins of lakes and streams, far from being hidden like those of most birds, are conspicuously large, and conical in shape like Indian wigwams. They are built of plants – rushes, sedges, mosses, etc – and ornamented around the base with mussel-shells. It was always pleasant and interesting to see them in the fall as soon as the nights began to be frosty, hard at work cutting sedges on the edge of the meadow or swimming out through the rushes, making long glittering ripples as they sculled themselves along, diving where the water is perhaps six or eight feet deep and reappearing in a minute or so with large mouthfuls of the weedy tangled plants gathered from the bottom, returning to their big wigwams climbing up and depositing their loads where most needed to make them yet larger and firmer and warmer, foreseeing the freezing weather just like ourselves when we banked up our house to keep out the frost.

They lie snug and invisible all winter but do not hibernate. Through a channel carefully kept open they swim out under the ice for mussels, and the roots and stems of water-lilies, etc., on which they feed just as they do in summer. Sometimes the oldest and most enterprising of them venture to orchards near the water in search of fallen apples; very seldom, however, do they interfere with anything belonging to their mortal enemy, man. Notwithstanding they are so well hidden and protected during the winter, many of them are killed by Indian hunters, who creep up softly and spear them through the thick walls of their cabins. Indians are fond of their flesh, and so are some of the wildest of the white trappers. They are easily caught in steel traps, and after vainly trying to drag their feet from the cruel crushing jaws, they sometimes in their agony gnaw them off. Even after having gnawed off a leg they are so guileless that they never seem to learn to know and fear traps, for some are occasionally found that have been caught twice and have gnawed off a second foot. Many other animals suffering excruciating pain in these cruel traps gnaw off their legs. Crabs and lobsters are so fortunate as to be able to shed their limbs when caught or merely frightened, apparently without suffering any pain, simply by giving themselves a little shivery shake.

The muskrat is one of the most notable and widely distributed of American animals, and millions of the gentle, industrious, beaver-like creatures are shot and trapped and speared every season for their skins, worth a dime or so – like shooting boys and girls for their garments.

Surely a better time must be drawing nigh when godlike human beings will become truly humane, and learn to put their animal fellow mortals in their hearts instead of on their backs or in their dinners. In the meantime we may just as well as not learn to live clean, innocent lives instead of slimy, bloody ones. All hale, red-blooded boys are savage, the best and boldest the savagest, fond of hunting and fishing. But when thoughtless childhood is past, the best rise the highest above all this bloody flesh and sport business, the wild foundational animal dying out day by day, as divine uplifting, transfiguring charity grows in.

Hares and rabbits were seldom seen when we first settled in the Wisconsin woods, but they multiplied rapidly after the animals that preyed upon them had been thinned out or exterminated, and food and shelter supplied in grain-fields and log fences and the thickets of young oaks that grew up in pastures after the annual grass fires were kept out. Catching hares in the winter-time, when they were hidden in hollow fence-logs, was a favorite pastime with many of the boys whose fathers allowed them time to enjoy the sport. Occasionally a stout, lithe hare was carried out into an open snow-covered field, set free, and given a chance for its life in a race with a dog. When the snow was not too soft and deep, it usually made good its escape, for our dogs were only fat, short-legged mongrels. We sometimes discovered hares in standing hollow trees, crouching on decayed punky wood at the bottom, as far back as possible from the opening, but when alarmed they managed to climb to a considerable height if the hollow was not too wide, by bracing themselves against the sides.

Foxes, though not uncommon, we boys held steadily to work seldom saw, and as they found plenty of prairie chickens for themselves and families, they did not often come near the farmer's hen-roosts. Nevertheless the discovery of their dens was considered important. No matter how deep the den might be, it was thoroughly explored with pick and shovel by sport-loving settlers at a time when they judged the fox was likely to be at home, but I cannot remember any case in our neighborhood where the fox was actually captured. In one of the dens a mile or two from our farm a lot of prairie chickens were found and some smaller birds.

Badger dens were far more common than fox dens. One of our fields was named Badger Hill from the number of badger holes in a hill at the end of it, but I cannot remember seeing a single one of the inhabitants.

On a stormy day in the middle of an unusually severe winter, a black bear, hungry, no doubt, and seeking something to eat, came strolling down through our neighborhood from the northern pine woods. None had been seen here before, and it caused no little excitement and alarm, for the European settlers imagined that these poor, timid, bashful bears were as dangerous as man-eating lions and tigers, and that they would pursue any human being that came in their way. This species is common in the north part of the State, and few of our enterprising Yankee hunters who went to the pineries in the fall failed to shoot at least one of them.

We saw very little of the owlish, serious looking coons, and no wonder, since they lie hidden nearly all day in hollow trees and we never had time to hunt them. We often heard their curious, quavering, whinnying cries on still evenings but only once succeeded in tracing an unfortunate family through our corn-field to their den in a big oak and catching them all. One of our neighbors, Mr McRath, a Highland Scotchman, caught one and made a pet of it. It became very tame and had perfect confidence in the good intentions of its kind friend and master. He always addressed it in speaking to it as a 'little man.' When it came running to him and jumped on his lap or climbed up his trousers, he would say, while patting its head as if it were a dog or a child, 'Coonie, ma mannie, Coonie, ma mannie, hoo are ye the day? I think you're hungry,' – as the comical pet began to examine his pockets for nuts and bits of bread – 'Na, na, there's nathing in my pooch for ye the day, my wee mannie, but I'll get ye something.' He would then fetch something it liked – bread, nuts, a carrot, or perhaps a piece of fresh meat. Anything scattered for it on the floor it felt with its paw instead of looking at it, judging of its worth more by touch than sight.

The outlet of our Fountain Lake flowed past Mr McRath's door, and the coon was very fond of swimming in it and searching for frogs and mussels. It seemed perfectly satisfied to stay about the house without being confined, occupied a comfortable bed in a section of a hollow tree, and never wandered far. How long it lived after the death of its kind master I don't know.

I suppose that almost any wild animal may be made a pet, simply by sympathizing with it and entering as much as possible into its life. In Alaska I saw one of the common gray mountain marmots kept as a pet in an Indian family. When its master entered the house it always seemed glad, almost like a dog, and when cold or tired it snuggled up in a fold of his blanket with the utmost confidence.

We have all heard of ferocious animals, lions and tigers, etc., that were fed and spoken to only by their masters, becoming perfectly tame; and, as is well known, the faithful dog that follows man and serves him, and looks up to him and loves him as if he were a god, is a descendant of the blood-thirsty wolf or jackal. Even frogs and toads and fishes may be tamed, provided they have the uniform sympathy of one person, with whom they become intimately acquainted without the distracting and varying attentions of strangers. And surely all God's people, however serious and savage, great or small, like to play. Whales and elephants, dancing, humming gnats, and invisibly small mischievous microbes – all are warm with divine radium and must have lots of fun in them.

As far as I know, all wild creatures keep themselves clean. Birds, it seems to me, take more pains to bathe and dress themselves than any other animals. Even ducks, though living so much in water, dip and scatter cleansing showers over their backs, and shake and preen their feathers as carefully as land-birds. Watching small singers taking their morning baths is very interesting, particularly when the weather is cold. Alighting in a shallow pool, they often-times show a sort of dread of dipping into it, like children hesitating about taking a plunge, as if they felt the same kind of shock, and this makes it easy for us to sympathize with the little feathered people.

Occasionally I have seen from my study-window red-headed linnets bathing in dew when water elsewhere was scarce. A large Monterey cypress with broad branches and innumerable leaves on which the dew lodges in still nights made favorite bathing-places. Alighting gently, as if afraid to waste the dew, they would pause and fidget as they do before beginning to plash in pools, then dip and scatter the drops in showers and get as thorough a bath as they would in a pool. I have also seen the same kind of baths taken by birds on the boughs of silver firs on the edge of a glacier meadow, but nowhere have I seen the dew-drops so abundant as on the Monterey cypress; and the picture made by the quivering wings and irised dew was memorably beautiful. Children, too, make fine pictures plashing and crowing in their little tubs. How widely different from wallowing pigs, bathing with great show of comfort and rubbing themselves dry against rough-barked trees!

Some of our own species seem fairly to dread the touch of water. When the necessity of absolute cleanliness by means of frequent baths was being preached by a friend who had been reading Combe's Physiology, in which he had learned something of the wonders of the skin with its millions of pores that had to be kept open for health, one of our neighbors remarked: 'Oh! that's unnatural. It's well enough to wash in a tub maybe once or twice a year, but not to be paddling in the water all the time like a frog in a spring-hole.' Another neighbor, who prided himself on his knowledge of big words, said with great solemnity: 'I never can believe that man is amphibious!'

Natives of tropic islands pass a large part of their lives in water, and seem as much at home in the sea as on the land; swim and dive, pursue fishes, play in the waves like surf-ducks and seals, and explore the coral gardens and groves and seaweed meadows as if truly amphibious. Even the natives of the far north bathe at times. I once saw a lot of Eskimo boys ducking and plashing right merrily in the Arctic Ocean.

It seemed very wonderful to us that the wild animals could keep themselves warm and strong in winter when the temperature was far below zero. Feeble-looking rabbits scud away over the snow, lithe and elastic, as if glorying in the frosty, sparkling weather and sure of their dinners. I have seen gray squirrels dragging ears of corn about as heavy as themselves out of our field through loose snow and up a tree, balancing them on limbs and eating in comfort with their dry, electric tails spread airily over their backs. Once I saw a fine hardy fellow go into a knot-hole. Thrusting in my hand I caught him and pulled him out. As soon as he guessed what I was up to, he took the end of my thumb in his mouth and sunk his teeth right through it, but I gripped him hard by the neck, carried him home, and shut him up in a box that contained about half a bushel of hazel- and hickory-nuts, hoping that he would not be too much frightened and discouraged to eat while thus imprisoned after the rough handling he had suffered. I soon learned, however, that sympathy in this direction was wasted, for no sooner did I pop him in than he fell to with right hearty appetite, gnawing and munching the nuts as if he had gathered them himself and was very hungry that day. Therefore, after allowing time enough for a good square meal, I made haste to get him out of the nut-box and shut him up in a spare bedroom, in which Father had hung a lot of selected ears of Indian corn for seed. They were hung up by the husks on cords stretched across from side to side of the room. The squirrel managed to jump from the top of one of the bed-posts to the cord, cut off an ear, and let it drop to the floor. He then jumped down, got a good grip of the heavy ear, carried it to the top of one of the slippery, polished bed-posts, seated himself comfortably, and, holding it well balanced, deliberately pried out one kernel at a time with his long chisel teeth, ate the soft, sweet germ, and dropped the hard part of the kernel. In this masterly way, working at high speed, he demolished several ears a day, and with a good warm bed in a box made himself at home and grew fat. Then naturally, I suppose, free romping in the snow and treetops with companions came to mind. Anyhow he began to look for a way of escape. Of course he first tried the window, but found that his teeth made no impression on the glass. Next he tried the sash and gnawed the wood off level with the glass; then Father happened to come upstairs and discovered the mischief that was being done to his seed corn and window and immediately ordered him out of the house.

The flying squirrel was one of the most interesting of the little animals we found in the woods, a beautiful brown creature, with fine eyes and smooth, soft fur like that of a mole or field mouse. He is about half as long as the gray squirrel, but his wide-spread tail and the folds of skin along his sides that form the wings make him look broad and flat, something like a kite. In the evenings our cat often brought them to her kittens at the shanty, and later we saw them fly during the day from the trees we were chopping. They jumped and glided off smoothly and apparently without effort, like birds, as soon as they heard and felt the breaking shock of the strained fibers at the stump, when the trees they were in began to totter and groan. They can fly, or rather glide, twenty or thirty yards from the top of a tree twenty or thirty feet high to the foot of another, gliding upward as they reach the trunk, or if the distance is too great they alight comfortably on the ground and make haste to the nearest tree, and climb just like the wingless squirrels.

Every boy and girl loves the little fairy, airy striped chipmunk, half squirrel, half spermophile. He is about the size of a field mouse, and often made us think of linnets and song sparrows as he frisked about gathering nuts and berries. He likes almost all kinds of grain, berries, and nuts – hazel-nuts, hickory-nuts, strawberries, huckleberries, wheat, oats, corn – he is fond of them all and thrives on them. Most of the hazel bushes on our farm grew along the fences as if they had been planted for the chipmunks alone, for the rail fences were their favorite highways. We never wearied watching them, especially when the hazel-nuts were ripe and the little fellows were sitting on the rails nibbling and handling them like tree-squirrels. We used to notice too that, although they are very neat animals, their lips and fingers were dyed red like our own, when the strawberries and huckleberries were ripe. We could always tell when the wheat and oats were in the milk by seeing the chipmunks feeding on the ears. They kept nibbling at the wheat until it was harvested and then gleaned in the stubble, keeping up a careful watch for their enemies – dogs, hawks, and shrikes. They are as widely distributed over the continent as the squirrels, various species inhabiting different regions on the mountains and lowlands, but all the different kinds have the same general characteristics of light, airy cheerfulness and good nature.

Before the arrival of farmers in the Wisconsin woods the small ground squirrels, called 'gophers,' lived chiefly on the seeds of wild grasses and weeds, but after the country was cleared and ploughed no feasting animal fell to more heartily on the farmer's wheat and corn. Increasing rapidly in numbers and knowledge, they became very destructive, especially in the spring when the corn was planted, for they learned to trace the rows and dig up and eat the three or four seeds in each hill about as fast as the poor farmers could cover them. And unless great pains were taken to diminish the numbers of the cunning little robbers, the fields had to be planted two or three times over, and even then large gaps in the rows would be found. The loss of the grain they consumed after it was ripe, together with the winter stores laid up in their burrows, amounted to little as compared with the loss of the seed on which the whole crop depended.

One evening about sundown, when my father sent me out with the shotgun to hunt them in a stubble field, I learned something curious and interesting in connection with these mischievous gophers, though just then they were doing no harm. As I strolled through the stubble watching for a chance for a shot, a shrike flew past me and alighted on an open spot at the mouth of a burrow about thirty yards ahead of me. Curious to see what he was up to, I stood still to watch him. He looked down the gopher hole in a listening attitude, then looked back at me to see if I was coming, looked down again and listened, and looked back at me. I stood perfectly still, and he kept twitching his tail, seeming uneasy and doubtful about venturing to do the savage job that I soon learned he had in his mind. Finally, encouraged by my keeping so still, to my astonishment he suddenly vanished in the gopher hole.

A bird going down a deep narrow hole in the ground like a ferret or a weasel seemed very strange, and I thought it would be a fine thing to run forward, clap my hand over the hole, and have the fun of imprisoning him and seeing what he would do when he tried to get out. So I ran forward but stopped when I got within a dozen or fifteen yards of the hole, thinking it might perhaps be more interesting to wait and see what would naturally happen without my interference. While I stood there looking and listening, I heard a great disturbance going on in the burrow, a mixed lot of keen squeaking shrieking, distressful cries, telling that down in the dark something terrible was being done. Then suddenly out popped a half-grown gopher, four and a half or five inches long, and, without stopping a single moment to choose a way of escape, ran screaming through the stubble straight away from its home, quickly followed by another and another, until some half-dozen were driven out, all of them crying and running in different directions as if at this dreadful time home, sweet home, was the most dangerous and least desirable of any place in the wide world. Then out came the shrike, flew above the run-away gopher children, and, diving on them, killed them one after another with blows at the back of the skull. He then seized one of them, dragged it to the top of a small clod so as to be able to get a start, and laboriously made out to fly with it about ten or fifteen yards, when he alighted to rest. Then he dragged it to the top of another clod and flew with it about the same distance, repeating this hard work over and over again until he managed to get one of the gophers on to the top of a log fence. How much he ate of his hard-won prey, or what he did with the others, I can't tell, for by this time the sun was down and I had to hurry home to my chores.

Chapter 6
THE PLOUGHBOY

At first, wheat, corn, and potatoes were the principal crops we raised; wheat especially. But in four or five years the soil was so exhausted that only five or six bushels an acre, even in the better fields, was obtained, although when first ploughed twenty and twenty-five bushels was about the ordinary yield. More attention was then paid to corn, but without fertilizers the corn-crop also became very meager. At last it was discovered that English clover would grow on even the exhausted fields, and that when ploughed under and planted with corn, or even wheat, wonderful crops were raised. This caused a complete change in farming methods; the farmers raised fertilizing clover, planted corn, and fed the crop to cattle and hogs.

But no crop raised in our wilderness was so surprisingly rich and sweet and purely generous to us boys and, indeed, to everybody as the watermelons and muskmelons. We planted a large patch on a sunny hill-slope the very first spring, and it seemed miraculous that a few handfuls of little fat seeds should in a few months send up a hundred wagon-loads of crisp, sumptuous, red-hearted and yellow-hearted fruits covering all the hill. We soon learned to know when they were in their prime, and when over-ripe and mealy. Also that if a second crop was taken from the same ground without fertilizing it, the melons would be small and what we called soapy; that is, soft and smooth, utterly uncrisp, and without a trace of the lively freshness and sweetness of those raised on virgin soil. Coming in from the farm work at noon, the half-dozen or so of melons we had placed in our cold spring were a glorious luxury that only weary barefooted farm boys can ever know.

Spring was not very trying as to temperature, and refreshing rains fell at short intervals. The work of ploughing commenced as soon as the frost was out of the ground. Corn- and potato-planting and the sowing of spring wheat was comparatively light work, while the nesting birds sang cheerily, grass and flowers covered the marshes and meadows and all the wild, uncleared parts of the farm, and the trees put forth their new leases, those of the oaks forming beautiful purple masses as if every leaf were a petal; and with all this we enjoyed the mild soothing winds, the hung of innumerable small insects and hylas, and the freshness and fragrance of everything. Then, too, came the wonderful passenger pigeons streaming from the south, and flocks of geese and cranes, filling all the sky with whistling wings.

The summer work, on the contrary, was deadly heavy, especially harvesting and corn-hoeing. All the ground had to be hoed over for the first few years, before Father bought cultivators or small weed-covering ploughs, and we were not allowed a moment's rest. The hoes had to be kept working up and down as steadily as if they were moved by machinery. Ploughing for winter wheat was comparatively easy, when we walked barefooted in the furrows, while the fine autumn tints kindled in the woods, and the hillsides were covered with golden pumpkins.

In summer the chores were grinding scythes, feeding the animals, chopping stove-wood, and carrying water up the hill from the spring on the edge of the meadow, etc. Then breakfast, and to the harvest or hay-field. I was foolishly ambitious to be first in mowing and cradling, and by the time I was sixteen led all the hired men. An hour was allowed at noon for dinner and more chores; we stayed in the field until dark, then supper, and still more chores, family worship, and to bed; making altogether a hard, sweaty day of about sixteen or seventeen hours. Think of that, ye blessed eight-hour-day labourers!

In winter Father came to the foot of the stairs and called us at six o'clock to feed the horses and cattle, grind axes, bring in wood, and do any other chores required, then breakfast, and out to work in the mealy, frosty snow by daybreak, chopping, fencing, etc. So in general our winter work was about as restless and trying as that of the long-day summer. No matter what the weather, there was always something to do. During heavy rains or snow-storms we worked in the barn, shelling corn, fanning wheat, thrashing with the flail, making axe-handles or ox-yokes, mending things, or sprouting and sorting potatoes in the cellar.

No pains were taken to diminish or in any way soften the natural hardships of this pioneer farm life; nor did any of the Europeans seem to know how to find reasonable ease and comfort if they would. The very best oak and hickory fuel was embarrassingly abundant and cost nothing but cutting and common sense; but instead of hauling great heart-cheering loads of it for wide, open, all-welcoming, climate-changing, beauty-making, Godlike ingle-fires, it was hauled with weary heart-breaking industry into fences and waste places to get it out of the way of the plough, and out of the way of doing good. The only fire for the whole house was the kitchen stove, with a fire-box about eighteen inches long and eight inches wide and deep – scant space for three or four small sticks, around which in hard zero weather all the family of ten persons shivered, and beneath which in the morning we found our socks and coarse, soggy boots frozen solid. We were not allowed to start even this despicable little fire in its black box to thaw them. No, we had to squeeze our throbbing, aching, chilblained feet into them, causing greater pain than toothache, and hurry out to chores. Fortunately the miserable chilblain pain began to abate as soon as the temperature of our feet approached the freezing-point, enabling us in spite of hard work and hard frost to enjoy the winter beauty – the wonderful radiance of the snow when it was starry with crystals, and the dawns and the sunsets and white noons, and the cheery, enlivening company of the brave chickadees and nuthatches.

The winter stars far surpassed those of our stormy Scotland in brightness, and we gazed and gazed as though we had never seen stars before. Oftentimes the heavens were made still more glorious by auroras, the long lance rays, called 'Merry Dancers' in Scotland, streaming with startling tremulous motion to the zenith. Usually the electric auroral light is white or pale yellow, but in the third or fourth of our Wisconsin winters there was a magnificently colored aurora that was seen and admired over nearly all the continent. The whole sky was draped in graceful purple and crimson folds glorious beyond description. Father called us out into the yard in front of the house where we had a wide view, crying, 'Come! Come, Mother! Come, bairns! And see the glory of God. All the sky is clad in a robe of red light. Look straight up to the crown where the folds are gathered. Hush and wonder and adore, for surely this is the clothing of the Lord Himself, and perhaps He will even now appear looking down from his high heaven.' This celestial show was far more glorious than anything we had ever yet beheld, and throughout that wonderful winter hardly anything else was spoken of.

We even enjoyed the snowstorms, the thronging crystals, like daisies, coming down separate and distinct, were very different from the tufted flakes we enjoyed so much in Scotland, when we ran into the midst of the slow-falling feathery throng shouting with enthusiasm: 'Jennie's plucking her doos! Jennie's plucking her doos!' (doves).

Nature has many ways of thinning and pruning and trimming her forests – lightning-strokes, heavy snow, and storm-winds to shatter and blow down whole trees here and there or break off branches as required. The results of these methods I have observed in different forests, but only once have I seen pruning by rain. The rain froze on the trees as it fell and grew so thick and heavy that many of them lost a third or more of their branches. The view of the woods after the storm had passed and the sun shone forth was something never to be forgotten. Every twig and branch and rugged trunk was encased in pure crystal ice, and each oak and hickory and willow became a fairy crystal palace. Such dazzling brilliance, such effects of white light and irised light glowing and flashing I had never seen before, nor have I since. This sudden change of the leafless woods to glowing silver was, like the great aurora, spoken of for years, and is one of the most beautiful of the many pictures that enriches my life. And besides the great shows there were thousands of others even in the coldest weather manifesting the utmost fineness and tenderness of beauty and affording noble compensation for hardship and pain.

One of the most striking of the winter sounds was the loud roaring and rumbling of the ice on our lake, from its shrinking and expanding with the changes of the weather. The fishermen who were catching pickerel said that they had no luck when this roaring was going on above the fish. I remember how frightened we boys were when on one of our New Year holidays we were taking a walk on the ice and heard for the first time the sudden rumbling roar beneath our feet and running on ahead of us, creaking and whooping as if all the ice eighteen or twenty inches thick was breaking.

In the neighborhood of our Wisconsin farm there were extensive swamps consisting in great part of a thick sod of very tough carex roots covering thin, watery lakes of mud. They originated in glacier lakes that were gradually overgrown. This sod was so tough that oxen with loaded wagons could be driven over it without cutting down through it, although it was afloat. The carpenters who came to build our frame house, noticing how the sedges sunk beneath their feet, said that if they should break through, they would probably be well on their way to California before touching bottom. On the contrary, all these lake-basins are shallow as compared with their width. When we went into the Wisconsin woods there was not a single wheel-track or cattle-track. The only man-made road was an Indian trail along the Fox River between Portage and Packwauckee Lake. Of course the deer, foxes, badgers, coons, skunks, and even the squirrels had well-beaten tracks from their dens and hiding-places in thickets, hollow trees, and the ground, but they did not reach far, and but little noise was made by the soft-footed travelers in passing over them, only a slight rustling and swishing among fallen leaves and grass.

Corduroying the swamps formed the principal part of road-making among the early settlers for many a day. At these annual road-making gatherings opportunity was offered for discussion of the news, politics, religion, war, the state of the crops, comparative advantages of the new country over the old, and so forth, but the principal opportunities, recurring every week, were the hours after Sunday church services. I remember hearing long talks on the wonderful beauty of the Indian corn; the wonderful melons, so wondrous fine for 'sloken a body on hot days'; their contempt for tomatoes, so fine to look at with their sunny colors and so disappointing in taste; the miserable cucumbers the 'Yankee bodies' ate, though tasteless as rushes; the character of the Yankees, etcetera. Then there were long discussions about the Russian war, news of which was eagerly gleaned from Greeley's *New York Tribune*; the great battles of the Alma, the charges at Balaklava and Inkerman; the siege of Sebastopol; the military genius of Todleben; the character of Nicholas; the character of the Russian soldier, his stubborn bravery, who for the first time in history withstood the British bayonet charges; the probable outcome of the terrible war; the fate of Turkey, and so forth.

Very few of our old-country neighbors gave much heed to what are called spirit-rappings. On the contrary, they were regarded as a sort of sleight-of-hand humbug. Some of these spirits seem to be stout able-bodied fellows, judging by the weights they lift and the heavy furniture they bang about. But they do no good work that I know of; never saw wood, grind corn, cook, feed the hungry, or go to the help of poor sinuous mothers at the bedsides of their sick children. I noticed when I was a boy that it was not the strongest characters who followed so-called mediums. When a rapping-storm was at its height in Wisconsin, one of our neighbors, an old Scotchman, remarked, 'Thay puir silly medium-bodies may gang to the deil wi' their rappin' speerits, for they dae nae gude, and I think the deil's their fayther.'

Although in the spring of 1849 there was no other settler within a radius of four miles of our Fountain Luke farm, in three or four years almost every quarter-section of government land was taken up, mostly by enthusiastic home-seekers from Great Britain, with only here and there Yankee families from adjacent states, who had come drifting indefinitely westward in covered wagons, seeking their fortunes like winged seeds; all alike striking root and gripping the glacial drift soil as naturally as oak and hickory trees; happy and hopeful, establishing homes and making wider and wider fields in the hospitable wilderness. The axe and plough were kept very busy; cattle, horses, sheep, and pigs multiplied; barns and corn-cribs were filled up, and man and beast were well fed; a schoolhouse was built, which was used also for a church; and in a very short time the new country began to look like an old one.

Comparatively few of the first settlers suffered from serious accidents. One of our neighbors had a finger shot off, and on a bitter, frosty night had to be taken to a surgeon in Portage, in a sled drawn by slow, plodding oxen, to have the shattered stump dressed. Another fell from his wagon and was killed by the wheel passing over his body. An acre of ground was reserved and fenced for graves, and soon consumption came to fill it. One of the saddest instances was that of a Scotch family from Edinburgh, consisting of a father, son, and daughter, who settled on eighty acres of land within half a mile of our place. The daughter died of consumption the third year after their arrival, the son one or two years later, and at last the father followed his two children. Thus sadly ended bright hopes and dreams of a happy home in rich and free America.

Another neighbor, I remember, after a lingering illness died of the same disease in mid-winter, and his funeral was attended by the neighbors in sleighs during a driving snowstorm when the thermometer was fifteen or twenty degrees below zero. The great white plague carried off another of our near neighbors, a fine Scotchman, the father of eight promising boys, when he was only about forty-five years of age. Most of those who suffered from this disease seemed hopeful and cheerful up to a very short time before their death, but Mr Reid, I remember, on one of his last visits to our house, said with brave resignation: 'I know that never more in this world can I be well, but I must just submit. I must just submit.'

One of the saddest deaths from other causes than consumption was that of a poor feeble-minded man whose brother, a sturdy, devout, severe puritan, was a very hard taskmaster. Poor half-witted Charlie was kept steadily at work – although he was not able to do much, for his body was about as feeble as his mind. He never could be taught the right use of an axe, and when he was set to chopping down trees for firewood he feebly hacked and chipped round and round them, sometimes spending several days in nibbling down a tree that a beaver might have gnawed down in half the time. Occasionally when he had an extra large tree to chop, he would go home and report that the tree was too tough and strong for him and that he could never make it fall. Then his brother, calling him a useless creature, would fell it with a few well-directed strokes, and leave Charlie to nibble away at it for weeks trying to make it into stove-wood.

His guardian brother, delighting in hard work and able for anything, was as remarkable for strength of body and mind as poor Charlie for childishness. All the neighbors pitied Charlie, especially the women, who never missed an opportunity to give him kind words, cookies, and pie; above all, they bestowed natural sympathy on the poor imbecile as if he were an unfortunate motherless child. In particular, his nearest neighbors, Scotch Highlanders, warmly welcomed him to their home and never wearied in doing everything that tender sympathy could suggest. To those friends he ran gladly at every opportunity. But after years of suffering from overwork and illness his feeble health failed, and he told his Scotch friends one day that he was not able to work any more or do anything that his brother wanted him to do, that he was tired of life, and that he had come to thank them for their kindness and to bid them goodbye, for he was going to drown himself in Muir's lake. 'Oh, Charlie! Charlie!' they cried, 'you mustn't talk that way. Cheer up! You will soon be stronger. We all love you. Cheer up! Cheer up! And always come here whenever you need anything.'

'Oh, no! my friends,' he pathetically replied, 'I know you love me, but I can't cheer up any more. My heart's gone, and I want to die.'

Next day, when Mr Anderson, a carpenter whose house was on the west shore of our lake, was going to a spring he saw a man wade out through the rushes and lily-pads and throw himself forward into deep water. This was poor Charlie. Fortunately, Mr Anderson had a skiff close by, and as the distance was not great he reached the broken-hearted imbecile in time to save his life, and after trying to cheer him took him home to his brother. But even this terrible proof of despair failed to soften his brother. He seemed to regard the attempt at suicide simply as a crime calculated to bring harm to religion. Though snatched from the lake to his bed, poor Charlie lived only a few days longer. A physician who was called when his health first became seriously impaired reported that he was suffering from Bright's disease. After all was over, the stoical brother walked over to the neighbor who had saved Charlie from drowning, and, after talking on ordinary affairs, crops, the weather, etc., said in a careless tone: 'I have a little job of carpenter work for you, Mr Anderson.' 'What is it, Mr – – ?' 'I want you to make a coffin.' 'A coffin!' said the startled carpenter. 'Who is dead?' 'Charlie,' he coolly replied. All the neighbors were in tears over the poor child man's fate. But, strange to say, the brother who had faithfully cared for him controlled and concealed all his natural affection as incompatible with sound faith.

The mixed lot of settlers around us offered a favorable field for observation of the different kinds of people of our own race. We were swift to note the way they behaved, the differences in their religion and morals, and in their ways of drawing a living from the same kind of soil under the same general conditions; how they protected themselves from the weather; how they were influenced by new doctrines and old ones seen in new lights in preaching, lecturing, debating, bringing up their children, etc., and how they regarded the Indians, those first settlers and owners of the ground that was being made into farms.

I well remember my father's discussing with a Scotch neighbor, a Mr George Mair, the Indian question as to the rightful ownership of the soil. Mr Mair remarked one day that it was pitiful to see how the unfortunate Indians, children of Nature, living on the natural products of the soil, hunting, fishing, and even cultivating small corn-fields on the most fertile spots, were now being robbed of their lands and pushed ruthlessly back into narrower and narrower limits by alien races who were cutting off their means of livelihood. Father replied that surely it could never have been the intention of God to allow Indians to rove and hunt over so fertile a country and hold it forever in unproductive wildness, while Scotch and Irish and English farmers could put it to so much better use. Where an Indian required thousands of acres for his family, these acres in the hands of industrious, God-fearing farmers would support ten or a hundred times more people in a far worthier manner, while at the same time helping to spread the gospel.

Mr Mair urged that such farming as our first immigrants were practicing was in many ways rude and full of the mistakes of ignorance, yet, rude as it was, and ill-tilled as were most of our Wisconsin farms by unskillful, inexperienced settlers who had been merchants and mechanics and servants in the old countries, how should we like to have specially trained and educated farmers drive us out of our homes and farms, such as they were, making use of the same argument, that God could never have intended such ignorant, unprofitable, devastating farmers as we were to occupy land upon which scientific farmers could raise five or ten times as much on each acre as we did? And I well remember thinking that Mr Mair had the better side of the argument. It then seemed to me that, whatever the final outcome might be, it was at this stage of the fight only an example of the rule of might with but little or no thought for the right or welfare of the other fellow if he were the weaker; that 'they should take who had the power, and they should keep who can,' as Wordsworth makes the marauding Scottish Highlanders say.

Many of our old neighbors toiled and sweated and grubbed themselves into their graves years before their natural dying days, in getting a living on a quarter-section of land and vaguely trying to get rich, while bread and raiment might have been serenely won on less than a fourth of this land, and time gained to get better acquainted with God.

I was put to the plough at the age of twelve, when my head reached but little above the handles, and for many years I had to do the greater part of the ploughing. It was hard work for so small a boy; nevertheless, as good ploughing was exacted from me as if I were a man, and very soon I had to become a good ploughman, or rather ploughboy. None could draw a straighter furrow. For the first few years the work was particularly hard on account of the tree-stumps that had to be dodged. Later the stumps were all dug and chopped out to make way for the McCormick reaper, and because I proved to be the best chopper and stump-digger I had nearly all of it to myself. It was dull, hard work leaning over on my knees all day, chopping out those tough oak and hickory stumps, deep down below the crowns of the big roots. Some, though fortunately not many, were two feet or more in diameter.

And as I was the eldest boy, the greater part of all the other hard work of the farm quite naturally fell on me. I had to split rails for long lines of zigzag fences. The trees that were tall enough and straight enough to afford one or two logs ten feet long were used for rails, the others, too knotty or cross-grained, were disposed of in log and cordwood fences. Making rails was hard work and required no little skill. I used to cut and split a hundred a day from our short, knotty oak timber, swinging the axe and heavy mallet, often with sore hands, from early morning to night. Father was not successful as a rail-splitter. After trying the work with me a day or two, he in despair left it all to me. I rather liked it, for I was proud of my skill, and tried to believe that I was as tough as the timber I mauled, though this and other heavy jobs stopped my growth and earned for me the title 'Runt of the family.'

In those early days, long before the great labor-saving machines came to our help, almost everything connected with wheat-raising abounded in trying work – cradling in the long, sweaty dog-days, raking and binding, stacking, thrashing – and it often seemed to me that our fierce, over-industrious way of getting the grain from the ground was too closely connected with grave-digging. The staff of life, naturally beautiful, often-times suggested the gravedigger's spade. Men and boys, and in those days even women and girls, were cut down while cutting the wheat. The fat folk grew lean and the lean leaner, while the rosy cheeks brought from Scotland and other cool countries across the sea faded to yellow like the wheat. We were all made slaves through the vice of over-industry. The same was in great part true in making hay to keep the cattle and horses through the long winters. We were called in the morning at four o'clock and seldom got to bed before nine, making a broiling, seething day seventeen hours long loaded with heavy work, while I was only a small stunted boy; and a few years later my brothers David and Daniel and my older sisters had to endure about as much as I did. In the harvest dog-days and dog-nights and dog-mornings, when we arose from our clammy beds, our cotton shirts clung to our backs as wet with sweat as the bathing-suits of swimmers, and remained so all the long, sweltering days. In mowing and cradling, the most exhausting of all the farm work, I made matters worse by foolish ambition in keeping ahead of the hired men. Never a warning word was spoken of the dangers of over-work. On the contrary, even when sick we were held to our tasks as long as we could stand. Once in harvest-time I had the mumps and was unable to swallow any food except milk, but this was not allowed to make any difference, while I staggered with weakness and sometimes fell headlong among the sheaves. Only once was I allowed to leave the harvest-field – when I was stricken down with pneumonia. I lay gasping for weeks, but the Scotch are hard to kill and I pulled through. No physician was called, for Father was an enthusiast, and always said and believed that God and hard work were by far the best doctors.

None of our neighbors were so excessively industrious as Father; though nearly all of the Scotch, English, and Irish worked too hard, trying to make good homes and to lay up money enough for comfortable independence. Excepting small garden-patches, few of them had owned land in the old country. Here their craving land-hunger was satisfied, and they were naturally proud of their farms and tried to keep them as neat and clean and well-tilled as gardens. To accomplish this without the means for hiring help was impossible. Flowers were planted about the neatly kept log or frame houses; barnyards, granaries, etc., were kept in about as neat order as the homes, and the fences and corn-rows were rigidly straight. But every uncut weed distressed them; so also did every ungathered ear of grain, and all that was lost by birds and gophers; and this overcarefulness bred endless work and worry.

As for money, for many a year there was precious little of it in the country for anybody. Eggs sold at six cents a dozen in trade, and five-cent calico was exchanged at twenty-five cents a yard. Wheat brought fifty cents a bushel in trade. To get cash for it before the Portage Railway was built, it had to be hauled to Milwaukee, a hundred miles away. On the other hand, food was abundant – eggs, chickens, pigs, cattle, wheat, corn, potatoes, garden vegetables of the best, and wonderful melons as luxuries. No other wild country I have ever known extended a kinder welcome to poor immigrants. On the arrival in the spring, a log house could be built, a few acres ploughed, the virgin sod planted with corn, potatoes, etc., and enough raised to keep a family comfortably the very first year; and wild hay for cows and oxen grew in abundance on the numerous meadows. The American settlers were wisely content with smaller fields and less of everything, kept indoors during excessively hot or cold weather, rested when tired, went off fishing and hunting at the most favorable times and seasons of the day and year, gathered nuts and berries, and in general tranquilly accepted all the good things the fertile wilderness offered.

After eight years of this dreary work of clearing the Fountain Lake farm, fencing it and getting it in perfect order, building a frame house and the necessary outbuildings for the cattle and horses – after all this had been victoriously accomplished, and we had made out to escape with life – Father bought a half-section of wild land about four or five miles to the eastward and began all over again to clear and fence and break up other fields for a new farm doubling all the stunting, heartbreaking chopping, grubbing, stump-digging, rail-splitting, fence-building, barn-building, house-building, and so forth.

By this time I had learned to run the breaking plough. Most of these ploughs were very large, turning furrows from eighteen inches to two feet wide, and were drawn by four or five yoke of oxen. They were used only for the first ploughing, in breaking up the wild sod woven into a tough mass, chiefly by the cordlike roots of perennial grasses, reinforced by the tap-roots of oak and hickory bushes, called 'grubs,' some of which were more than a century old and four or five inches in diameter. In the hardest ploughing on the most difficult ground, the grubs were said to be as thick as the hair on a dog's back. If in good trim, the plough cut through and turned over these grubs as if the century-old wood were soft like the flesh of carrots and turnips; but if not in good trim the grubs promptly tossed the plough out of the ground. A stout Highland Scot, our neighbor, whose plough was in bad order and who did not know how to trim it, was vainly trying to keep it in the ground by main strength, while his son, who was driving and merrily whipping up the cattle, would cry encouragingly, 'Haud her in, Fayther! Haud her in!'

'But hoo i' the deil can I haud her in when she'll no *stop* in?' his perspiring father would reply, gasping for breath between each word. On the contrary, with the share and coulter sharp and nicely adjusted, the plough, instead of shying at every grub and jumping out, ran straight ahead without need of steering or holding, and gripped the ground so firmly that it could hardly be thrown out at the end of the furrow.

Our breaker turned a furrow two feet wide, and on our best land, where the sod was toughest, held so firm a grip that at the end of the field my brother, who was driving the oxen, had to come to my assistance in throwing it over on its side to be drawn around the end of the landing; and it was all I could do to set it up again. But I learned to keep that plough in such trim that after I got started on a new furrow I used to ride on the crossbar between the handles with my feet resting comfortably on the beam, without having to steady or steer it in any way on the whole length of the field, unless we had to go round a stump, for it sawed through the biggest grubs without flinching.

The growth of these grubs was interesting to me. When an acorn or hickory-nut had sent up its first season's sprout, a few inches long, it was burned off in the autumn grass fires; but the root continued to hold on to life, formed a callus over the wound and sent up one or more shoots the next spring. Next autumn these new shoots were burned off, but the root and calloused head, about level with the surface of the ground, continued to grow and send up more new shoots; and so on, almost every year until very old, probably far more than a century, while the tops, which would naturally have become tall broad-headed trees, were only mere sprouts seldom more than two years old. Thus the ground was kept open like a prairie, with only five or six trees to the acre, which had escaped the fire by having the good fortune to grow on a bare spot at the door of a fox or badger den, or between straggling grass-tufts wide apart on the poorest sandy soil.

The uniformly rich soil of the Illinois and Wisconsin prairies produced so close and tall a growth of grasses for fires that no tree could live on it. Had there been no fires, these fine prairies, so marked a feature of the country, would have been covered by the heaviest forests. As soon as the oak openings in our neighborhood were settled, and the farmers had prevented running grass-fires, the grubs grew up into trees and formed tall thickets so dense that it was difficult to walk through them and every trace of the sunny 'openings' vanished.

We called our second farm Hickory Hill, from its many fine hickory trees and the long gentle slope leading up to it. Compared with Fountain Lake farm it lay high and dry. The land was better, but it had no living water, no spring or stream or meadow or lake. A well ninety feet deep had to be dug, all except the first ten feet or so in fine-grained sandstone. When the sandstone was struck, my father, on the advice of a man who had worked in mines, tried to blast the rock; but from lack of skill the blasting went on very slowly, and Father decided to have me do all the work with mason's chisels, a long, hard job, with a good deal of danger in it. I had to sit cramped in a space about three feet in diameter, and wearily chip, chip, with heavy hammer and chisels from early morning until dark, day after day, for weeks and months. In the morning, Father and David lowered me in a wooden bucket by a windlass, hauled up what chips were left from the night before, then went away to the farm work and left me until noon, when they hoisted me out for dinner. After dinner I was promptly lowered again, the forenoon's accumulation of chips hoisted out of the way, and I was left until night.

One morning, after the dreary bore was about eighty feet deep, my life was all but lost in deadly choke-damp – carbonic acid gas that had settled at the bottom during the night. Instead of clearing away the chips as usual when I was lowered to the bottom, I swayed back and forth and began to sink under the poison. Father, alarmed that I did not make any noise, shouted, 'What's keeping you so still?' to which he got no reply. Just as I was settling down against the side of the wall, I happened to catch a glimpse of a branch of a bur-oak tree which leaned out over the mouth of the shaft. This suddenly awakened me, and to Father's excited shouting I feebly murmured, 'Take me out.' But when he began to hoist he found I was not in the bucket and in wild alarm shouted, 'Get in! Get in the bucket and hold on! Hold on!' Somehow I managed to get into the bucket, and that is all I remembered until I was dragged out, violently gasping for breath.

One of our near neighbors, a stone mason and miner by the name of William Duncan, came to see me, and after hearing the particulars of the accident he solemnly said: 'Weel, Johnnie, it's God's mercy that you're alive. Many a companion of mine have I seen dead with choke-damp, but none that I ever saw or heard of was so near to death in it as you were and escaped without help.' Mr Duncan taught Father to throw water down the shaft to absorb the gas, and also to drop a bundle of brush or hay attached to a light rope, dropping it again and again to carry down pure air and stir up the poison. When, after a day or two, I had recovered from the shock, Father lowered me again to my work, after taking the precaution to test the air with a candle and stir it up well with a brush-and-hay bundle. The weary hammer-and-chisel-chipping went on as before, only more slowly, until ninety feet down, when at last I struck a fine, hearty gush of water. Constant dropping wears away stone. So does constant chipping, while at the same time wearing away the chipper. Father never spent an hour in that well. He trusted me to sink it straight and plumb, and I did, and built a fine covered top over it, and swung two iron-bound buckets in it from which we all drank for many a day.

The honey-bee arrived in America long before we boys did, but several years passed ere we noticed any on our farm. The introduction of the honey-bee into flowery America formed a grand epoch in bee history. This sweet humming creature, companion and friend of the flowers, is now distributed over the greater part of the continent, filling countless hollows in rocks and trees with honey as well as the millions of hives prepared for them by honey-farmers, who keep and tend their flocks of sweet winged cattle, as shepherds keep sheep – a charming employment, 'like directing sunbeams,' as Thoreau says. The Indians call the honey-bee the white man's fly; and though they had long been acquainted with several species of bumblebees that yielded more or less honey, how gladly surprised they must have been when they discovered that, in the hollow trees where before they had found only coons or squirrels, they found swarms of brown flies with fifty or even a hundred pounds of honey sealed up in beautiful cells. With their keen hunting senses they of course were not slow to learn the habits of the little brown immigrants and the best methods of tracing them to their sweet homes, however well hidden. During the first few years none were seen on our farm, though we sometimes heard Father's hired men talking about 'lining bees.' None of us boys ever found a bee tree, or tried to find any until about ten years after our arrival in the woods. On the Hickory Hill farm there is a ridge of moraine material, rather dry, but flowery with goldenrods and asters of many species, upon which we saw bees feeding in the late autumn just when their hives were fullest of honey, and it occurred to me one day after I was of age and my own master that I must try to find a bee tree. I made a little box about six inches long and four inches deep and wide; bought half a pound of honey, went to the goldenrod hill, swept a bee into the box and closed it. The lid had a pane of glass in it so I could see when the bee had sucked its fill and was ready to go home. At first it groped around trying to get out, but, smelling the honey, it seemed to forget everything else, and while it was feasting I carried the box and a small sharp-pointed stake to an open spot, where I could see about me, fixed the stake in the ground, and placed the box on the flat top of it. When I thought that the little feaster must be about full, I opened the box, but it was in no hurry to fly. It slowly crawled up to the edge of the box, lingered a minute or two cleaning its legs that had become sticky with honey, and when it took wing, instead of making what is called a bee-line for home, it buzzed around the box and minutely examined it as if trying to fix a clear picture of it in its mind so as to be able to recognize it when it returned for another load, then circled around at a little distance as if looking for something to locate it by. I was the nearest object, and the thoughtful worker buzzed in front of my face and took a good stare at me, and then flew up on to the top of an oak on the side of the open spot in the centre of which the honey-box was. Keeping a keen watch, after a minute or two of rest or wing-cleaning, I saw it fly in wide circles round the tops of the trees nearest the honey-box, and, after apparently satisfying itself, make a bee-line for the hive. Looking endwise on the line of flight, I saw that what is called a bee-line is not an absolutely straight line, but a line in general straight made of many slight, wavering, lateral curves. After taking as true a bearing as I could, I waited and watched. In a few minutes, probably ten, I was surprised to see that bee arrive at the end of the outleaning limb of the oak mentioned above, as though that was the first point it had fixed in its memory to be depended on in retracing the way back to the honey-box. From the tree-top it came straight to my head, thence straight to the box, entered without the least hesitation, filled up and started off after the same preparatory dressing and taking of bearings as before. Then I took particular pains to lay down the exact course so I would be able to trace it to the hive. Before doing so, however, I made all experiment to test the worth of the impression I had that the little insect found the way back to the box by fixing telling points in its mind. While it was away, I picked up the honey-box and set it on the stake a few rods from the position it had thus far occupied, and stood there watching. In a few minutes I saw the bee arrive at its guide-mark, the overleaning branch on the tree-top, and thence come bouncing down right to the spaces in the air which had been occupied by my head and the honey-box, and when the cunning little honey-gleaner found nothing there but empty air it whirled round and round as if confused and lost; and although I was standing with the open honey-box within fifty or sixty feet of the former feasting-spot, it could not, or at least did not, find it.

Now that I had learned the general direction of the hive, I pushed on in search of it. I had gone perhaps a quarter of a mile when I caught another bee, which, after getting loaded, went through the same performance of circling round and round the honey-box, buzzing in front of me and staring me in the face to be able to recognize me; but as if the adjacent trees and bushes were sufficiently well known, it simply looked around at them and bolted off without much dressing, indicating, I thought, that the distance to the hive was not great. I followed on and very soon discovered it in the bottom log of a corn-field fence, but some lucky fellow had discovered it before me and robbed it. The robbers had chopped a large hole in the log, taken out most of the honey, and left the poor bees late in the fall, when winter was approaching, to make haste to gather all the honey they could from the latest flowers to avoid starvation in the winter.

Chapter 7
KNOWLEDGE AND INVENTIONS

I learned arithmetic in Scotland without understanding any of
it, though I had the rules by heart. But when I was about fifteen
or sixteen years of age, I began to grow hungry for real
knowledge, and persuaded Father, who was willing enough
to have me study provided my farm work was kept up, to buy
me a higher arithmetic. Beginning at the beginning, in one
summer I easily finished it without assistance in the short
intervals between the end of dinner and the afternoon start for
the harvest-and-hay-fields, accomplishing more without a
teacher in a few scraps of time than in years in school before
my mind was ready for such work. Then in succession I took
up algebra, geometry, and trigonometry and made some little
progress in each, and reviewed grammar. I was fond of reading, but Father had brought only a few religious books from
Scotland. Fortunately, several of our neighbors had brought a
dozen or two of all sorts of books, which I borrowed and read,
keeping all of them except the religious ones carefully hidden
from Father's eye. Among these were Scott's novels, which,
like all other novels, were strictly forbidden, but devoured with
glorious pleasure in secret. Father was easily persuaded to buy
Josephus's 'Wars of the Jews,' and D'Aubigné's 'History of the
Reformation,' and I tried hard to get him to buy Plutarch's
Lives, which, as I told him, everybody, even religious people,
praised as a grand good book; but he would have nothing to
do with the old pagan until the graham bread and anti-flesh
doctrines came suddenly into our backwoods neighborhood,
making a stir something like phrenology and spirit-rappings,

which were as mysterious in their attacks as influenza. He then thought it possible that Plutarch might be turned to account on the food question by revealing what those old Greeks and Romans ate to make them strong; and so at last we gained our glorious Plutarch. Dick's 'Christian Philosopher,' which I borrowed from a neighbor, I thought I might venture to read in the open, trusting that the word 'Christian' would be proof against its cautious condemnation. But Father balked at the word 'Philosopher,' and quoted from the Bible a verse which spoke of 'philosophy falsely so-called.' I then ventured to speak in defense of the book, arguing that we could not do without at least a little of the most useful kinds of philosophy.

'Yes, we can,' he said with enthusiasm, 'the Bible is the only book human beings can possibly require throughout all the journey from earth to heaven.'

'But how,' I contended, 'can we find the way to heaven without the Bible, and how after we grow old can we read the Bible without a little helpful science? Just think, Father, you cannot read your Bible without spectacles, and millions of others are in the same fix; and spectacles cannot be made without some knowledge of the science of optics.'

'Oh!' he replied, perceiving the drift of the argument, 'there will always be plenty of worldly people to make spectacles.'

To this I stubbornly replied with a quotation from the Bible with reference to the time coming when 'all shall know the Lord from the least even to the greatest,' and then who will make the spectacles? But he still objected to my reading that book, called me a contumacious quibbler too fond of disputation, and ordered me to return it to the accommodating owner. I managed, however, to read it later.

On the food question Father insisted that those who argued for a vegetable diet were in the right, because our teeth showed plainly that they were made with reference to fruit and grain and not for flesh like those of dogs and wolves and tigers. He therefore promptly adopted a vegetable diet and requested Mother to make the bread from graham flour instead of bolted flour. Mother put both kinds on the table, and meat also, to let all the family take their choice, and while Father was insisting on the foolishness of eating flesh, I came to her help by calling Father's attention to the passage in the Bible which told the story of Elijah the prophet who, when he was pursued by enemies who wanted to take his life, was hidden by the Lord by the brook Cherith, and fed by ravens; and surely the Lord knew what was good to eat, whether bread or meat. And on what, I asked, did the Lord feed Elijah? On vegetables or graham bread? No, he directed the ravens to feed his prophet on flesh. The Bible being the sole rule, Father at once acknowledged that he was mistaken. The Lord never would have sent flesh to Elijah by the ravens if graham bread were better.

I remember as a great and sudden discovery that the poetry of the Bible, Shakespeare, and Milton was a source of inspiring, exhilarating, uplifting pleasure; and I became anxious to know all the poets, and saved up small sums to buy as many of their books as possible. Within three or four years I was the proud possessor of parts of Shakespeare's, Milton's, Cowper's, Henry Kirke White's, Campbell's, and Akenside's works, and quite a number of others seldom read nowadays. I think it was in my fifteenth year that I began to relish good literature with enthusiasm, and smack my lips over favorite lines, but there was desperately little time for reading, even in the winter evenings – only a few stolen minutes now and then. Father's strict rule was, straight to bed immediately after family worship, which in winter was usually over by eight o'clock. I was in the habit of lingering in the kitchen with a book and candle after the rest of the family had retired, and considered myself fortunate if I got five minutes' reading before Father noticed the light and ordered me to bed; an order that of course I immediately obeyed. But night after night I tried to steal minutes in the same lingering way, and how keenly precious those minutes were, few nowadays can know. Father failed perhaps two or three times in a whole winter to notice my light for nearly ten minutes, magnificent golden blocks of time, long to be remembered like holidays or geological periods. One evening when I was reading Church history Father was particularly irritable, and called out with hope-killing emphasis, 'John, go to bed! Must I give you a separate order every night to get you to go to bed? Now, I will have no irregularity in the family; you *must* go when the rest go, and without my having to tell you.' Then, as an afterthought, as if judging that his words and tone of voice were too severe for so pardonable an offense as reading a religious book, he unwarily added: 'If you *will* read, get up in the morning and read. You may get up in the morning as early as you like.'

That night I went to bed wishing with all my heart and soul that somebody or something might call me out of sleep to avail myself of this wonderful indulgence; and next morning to my joyful surprise I awoke before Father called me. A boy sleeps soundly after working all day in the snowy woods, but that frosty morning I sprang out of bed as if called by a trumpet blast, rushed downstairs, scarce feeling my chilblains, enormously eager to see how much time I had won; and when I held up my candle to a little clock that stood on a bracket in the kitchen I found that it was only one o'clock. I had gained five hours, almost half a day! 'Five hours to myself!' I said, 'five huge, solid hours!' I can hardly think of any other event in my life, any discovery I ever made that gave birth to joy so transportingly glorious as the possession of these five frosty hours.

In the glad, tumultuous excitement of so much suddenly acquired time-wealth, I hardly knew what to do with it. I first thought of going on with my reading, but the zero weather would make a fire necessary, and it occurred to me that Father might object to the cost of fire-wood that took time to chop. Therefore, I prudently decided to go down to the cellar, and begin work on a model of a self-setting sawmill I had invented. Next morning I managed to get up at the same gloriously early hour, and though the temperature of the cellar was a little below the freezing point, and my light was only a tallow candle, the mill work went joyfully on. There were a few tools in a corner of the cellar – a vise, files, a hammer, chisels, etc., that Father had brought from Scotland, but no saw excepting a coarse crooked one that was unfit for sawing dry hickory or oak. So I made a fine-tooth saw suitable for my work out of a strip of steel that had formed part of an old-fashioned corset, that cut the hardest wood smoothly. I also made my own bradawls, punches, and a pair of compasses, out of wire and old files.

My workshop was immediately under Father's bed, and the filing and tapping in making cogwheels, journals, cams, etc., must, no doubt, have annoyed him, but with the permission he had granted in his mind, and doubtless hoping that I would soon tire of getting up at one o'clock, he impatiently waited about two weeks before saying a word. I did not vary more than five minutes from one o'clock all winter, nor did I feel any bad effects whatever, nor did I think at all about the subject as to whether so little sleep might be in any way injurious; it was a grand triumph of will-power over cold and common comfort and work-weariness in abruptly cutting down my ten hours' allowance of sleep to five. I simply felt that I was rich beyond anything I could have dreamed of or hoped for. I was far more than happy. Like Tam o'Shanter I was 'glorious, O'er a' the ills o' life victorious.'

Father, as was customary in Scotland, gave thanks and asked a blessing before meals, not merely as a matter of form and decent Christian manners, for he regarded food as a gift derived directly from the hands of the Father in heaven. Therefore every meal to him was a sacrament requiring conduct and attitude of mind not unlike that befitting the Lord's Supper. No idle word was allowed to be spoken at our table, much less any laughing or fun or story-telling. When we were at the breakfast-table, about two weeks after the great golden time-discovery, Father cleared his throat preliminary, as we all knew, to saying something considered important. I feared that it was to be on the subject of my early rising, and dreaded the withdrawal of the permission he had granted on account of the noise I made, but still hoping that, as he had given his word that I might get up as early as I wished, he would as a Scotchman stand to it, even though it was given in an unguarded moment and taken in a sense unreasonably far-reaching. The solemn sacramental silence was broken by the dreaded question: –

'John, what time is it when you get up in the morning?'

'About one o'clock,' I replied in a low, meek, guilty tone of voice.

'And what kind of a time is that, getting up in the middle of the night and disturbing the whole family?'

I simply reminded him of the permission he had freely granted me to get up as early as I wished.

'I *know* it,' he said, in an almost agonized tone of voice, 'I *know* I gave you that miserable permission, but I never imagined that you would get up in the middle of the night.'

To this I cautiously made no reply, but continued to listen for the heavenly one-o'clock call, and it never failed.

After completing my self-setting sawmill I dammed one of the streams in the meadow and put the mill in operation. This invention was speedily followed by a lot of others – waterwheels, curious doorlocks and latches, thermometers, hygrometers, pyrometers, clocks, a barometer, an automatic contrivance for feeding the horses at any required hour, a lamplighter and fire-lighter, an early-or-late-rising machine, and so forth.

After the sawmill was proved and discharged from my mind, I happened to think it would be a fine thing to make a timekeeper which would tell the day of the week and the day of the month, as well as strike like a common clock and point out the hours; also to have an attachment whereby it could be connected with a bedstead to set me on my feet at any hour in the morning; also to start fires, light lamps, etc. I had learned the time laws of the pendulum from a book, but with this exception I knew nothing of timekeepers, for I had never seen the inside of any sort of clock or watch. After long brooding, the novel clock was at length completed in my mind, and was tried and found to be durable and to work well and look well before I had begun to build it in wood. I carried small parts of it in my pocket to whittle at when I was out at work on the farm using every spare or stolen moment within reach without Father's knowing anything about it. In the middle of summer, when harvesting was in progress, the novel time-machine was nearly completed. It was hidden upstairs in a spare bedroom where some tools were kept. I did the making and mending on the farm, but one day at noon, when I happened to be away, Father went upstairs for a hammer or something and discovered the mysterious machine back of the bedstead. My sister Margaret saw him on his knees examining it, and at the first opportunity whispered in my ear, 'John, Fayther saw that thing you're making upstairs.' None of the family knew what I was doing, but they knew very well that all such work was frowned on by Father, and kindly warned me of any danger that threatened my plans. The fine invention seemed doomed to destruction before its time-ticking commenced, though I thought it handsome, had so long carried it in my mind, and like the nest of Burns's wee mousie it had cost me mony a weary whittling nibble. When we were at dinner several days after the sad discovery, Father began to clear his throat to speak, and I feared the doom of martyrdom was about to be pronounced on my grand clock.

'John,' he inquired, 'what is that thing you are making upstairs?'

I replied in desperation that I didn't know what to call it.

'What! You mean to say you don't know what you are trying to do?'

'Oh, yes,' I said, 'I know very well what I am doing.'

'What, then, is the thing for?'

'It's for a lot of things,' I replied, 'but getting people up early in the morning is one of the main things it is intended for; therefore it might perhaps be called an early-rising machine.'

After getting up so extravagantly early all the last memorable winter, to make a machine for getting up perhaps still earlier seemed so ridiculous that he very nearly laughed. But after controlling himself and getting command of a sufficiently solemn face and voice he said severely, 'Do you not think it is very wrong to waste your time on such nonsense?'

'No,' I said meekly, 'I don't think I'm doing any wrong.'

'Well,' he replied, 'I assure you I do; and if you were only half as zealous in the study of religion as you are in contriving and whittling these useless, nonsensical things, it would be infinitely better for you. I want you to be like Paul, who said that he desired to know nothing among men but Christ and Him crucified.'

To this I made no reply, gloomily believing my fine machine was to be burned, but still taking what comfort I could in realizing that anyhow I had enjoyed inventing and making it.

After a few days, finding that nothing more was to be said, and that Father after all had not had the heart to destroy it, all necessity for secrecy being ended, I finished it in the half-hours that we had at noon and set it in the parlor between two chairs, hung moraine boulders that had come from the direction of Lake Superior on it for weights, and set it running. We were then hauling grain into the barn. Father at this period devoted himself entirely to the Bible and did no farm work whatever. The clock had a good loud tick, and when he heard it strike, one of my sisters told me that he left his study, went to the parlor, got down on his knees and carefully examined the machinery, which was all in plain sight, not being enclosed in a case. This he did repeatedly, and evidently seemed a little proud of my ability to invent and whittle such a thing, though careful to give no encouragement for anything more of the kind in future.

But somehow it seemed impossible to stop. Inventing and whittling faster than ever, I made another hickory clock, shaped like a scythe to symbolize the scythe of Father Time. The pendulum is a bunch of arrows symbolizing the flight of time. It hangs on a leafless mossy oak snag showing the effect of time, and on the snath is written, 'All flesh is grass.' This, especially the inscription, rather pleased Father, and, of course, Mother and all my sisters and brothers admired it. Like the first it indicates the days of the week and month, starts fires and beds at any given hour and minute, and, though made more than fifty years ago, is still a good timekeeper.

My mind still running on clocks, I invented a big one like a town clock with four dials, with the time-figures so large they could be read by all our immediate neighbors as well as ourselves when at work in the fields, and on the side next the house the days of the week and month were indicated. It was to be placed on the peak of the barn roof. But just as it was all but finished, Father stopped me, saying that it would bring too many people around the barn. I then asked permission to put it on the top of a black-oak tree near the house. Studying the larger main branches, I thought I could secure a sufficiently rigid foundation for it, while the trimmed sprays and leaves would conceal the angles of the cabin required to shelter the works from the weather, and the two-second pendulum, fourteen feet long, could be snugly encased on the side of the trunk. Nothing about the grand, useful timekeeper, I argued, would disfigure the tree, for it would look something like a big hawk's nest. 'But that,' he objected, 'would draw still bigger bothersome trampling crowds about the place, for whoever heard of anything so queer as a big clock on the top of a tree?' So I had to lay aside its big wheels and cams and rest content with the pleasure of inventing it, and looking at it in my mind and listening to the deep solemn throbbing of its long two-second pendulum with its two old axes back to back for the bob.

One of my inventions was a large thermometer made of an iron rod, about three feet long and five eighths of an inch in diameter, that had formed part of a wagon-box. The expansion and contraction of this rod was multiplied by a series of levers made of strips of hoop iron. The pressure of the rod against the levers was kept constant by a small counterweight, so that the slightest change in the length of the rod was instantly shown on a dial about three feet wide multiplied about thirty-two thousand times. The zero-point was gained by packing the rod in wet snow. The scale was so large that the big black hand on the white-painted dial could be seen distinctly and the temperature read while we were ploughing in the field below the house. The extremes of heat and cold caused the hand to make several revolutions. The number of these revolutions was indicated on a small dial marked on the larger one. This thermometer was fastened on the side of the house, and was so sensitive that when anyone approached it within four or five feet the heat radiated from the observer's body caused the hand of the dial to move so fast that the motion was plainly visible, and when he stepped back, the hand moved slowly back to its normal position. It was regarded as a great wonder by the neighbors and even by my own all-Bible father.

Boys are fond of the books of travelers, and I remember that one day, after I had been reading Mungo Park's travels in Africa, Mother said: 'Weel, John, maybe you will travel like Park and Humboldt some day.' Father overheard her and cried out in solemn deprecation, 'Oh, Anne! dinna put sic notions in the laddie's heed.' But at this time there was precious little need of such prayers. My brothers left the farm when they came of age, but I stayed a year longer, loath to leave home. Mother hoped I might be a minister some day; my sisters that I would be a great inventor. I often thought I should like to be a physician, but I saw no way of making money and getting the necessary education, excepting as an inventor. So, as a beginning, I decided to try to get into a big shop or factory and live awhile among machines. But I was naturally extremely shy and had been taught to have a poor opinion of myself, as of no account, though all our neighbors encouragingly called me a genius, sure to rise in the world. When I was talking over plans one day with a friendly neighbor, he said: 'Now, John, if you wish to get into a machine-shop, just take some of your inventions to the State Fair, and you may be sure that as soon as they are seen they will open the door of any shop in the country for you. You will be welcomed everywhere.' And when I doubtingly asked if people would care to look at things made of wood, he said, 'Made of wood! Made of wood! What does it matter what they're made of when they are so out-and-out original. There's nothing else like them in the world. That is what will attract attention, and besides they're mighty handsome things anyway to come from the backwoods.' So I was encouraged to leave home and go at his direction to the State Fair when it was being held in Madison.

Chapter 8

THE WORLD AND THE UNIVERSITY

When I told Father that I was about to leave home, and inquired whether, if I should happen to be in need of money, he would send me a little, he said, 'No; depend entirely on yourself.' Good advice, I suppose, but surely needlessly severe for a bashful, home-loving boy who had worked so hard. I had the gold sovereign that my grandfather had given me when I left Scotland, and a few dollars, perhaps ten, that I had made by raising a few bushels of grain on a little patch of sandy abandoned ground. So when I left home to try the world I had only about fifteen dollars in my pocket.

Strange to say, Father carefully taught us to consider ourselves very poor worms of the dust, conceived in sin, etc., and devoutly believed that quenching every spark of pride and self-confidence was a sacred duty, without realizing that in so doing he might at the same time be quenching everything else. Praise he considered most venomous, and tried to assure me that when I was fairly out in the wicked world making my own way I would soon learn that although I might have thought him a hard taskmaster at times, strangers were far harder. On the contrary, I found no lack of kindness and sympathy. All the baggage I carried was a package made up of the two clocks and a small thermometer made of a piece of old washboard, all three tied together, with no covering or case of any sort, the whole looking like one very complicated machine.

The aching parting from Mother and my sisters was, of course, hard to bear. Father let David drive me down to Pardeeville, a place I had never before seen, though it was only nine miles south of the Hickory Hill home. When we arrived at the village tavern, it seemed deserted. Not a single person was in sight. I set my clock baggage on the rickety platform. David said goodbye and started for home, leaving me alone in the world. The grinding noise made by the wagon in turning short brought out the landlord, and the first thing that caught his eye was my strange bundle. Then he looked at me and said, 'Hello, young man, what's this?'

'Machines,' I said, 'for keeping time and getting up in the morning, and so forth.'

'Well! Well! That's a mighty queer get-up. You must be a Down-East Yankee. Where did you get the pattern for such a thing?'

'In my head,' I said.

Someone down the street happened to notice the landlord looking intently at something and came up to see what it was. Three or four people in that little village formed an attractive crowd, and in fifteen or twenty minutes the greater part of the population of Pardeeville stood gazing in a circle around my strange hickory belongings. I kept outside of the circle to avoid being seen, and had the advantage of hearing the remarks without being embarrassed. Almost every one as he came up would say, 'What's that? What's it for? Who made it?' The landlord would answer them all alike, 'Why, a young man that lives out in the country somewhere made it, and he says it's a thing for keeping time, getting up in the morning, and something that I didn't understand. I don't know what he meant.' 'Oh, no!' one of the crowd would say, 'that can't be. It's for something else – something mysterious. Mark my words, you'll see all about it in the newspapers some of these days.' A curious little fellow came running up the street, joined the crowd, stood on tiptoe to get sight of the wonder, quickly made up his mind, and shouted in crisp, confident, cock-crowing style, 'I know what that contraption's for. It's a machine for taking the bones out of fish.'

This was in the time of the great popular phrenology craze, when the fences and barns along the roads throughout the country were plastered with big skull-bump posters, headed, 'Know Thyself,' and advising everybody to attend schoolhouse lectures to have their heads explained and be told what they were good for and whom they ought to marry. My mechanical bundle seemed to bring a good deal of this phrenology to mind, for many of the onlookers would say, 'I wish I could see that boy's head – he must have a tremendous bump of invention.' Others complimented me by saying, 'I wish I had that fellow's head. I'd rather have it than the best farm in the State.'

I stayed overnight at this little tavern, waiting for a train. In the morning I went to the station, and set my bundle on the platform. Along came the thundering train, a glorious sight, the first train I had ever waited for. When the conductor saw my queer baggage, he cried, 'Hello! What have we here?'

'Inventions for keeping time, early rising, and so forth. May I take them into the car with me?'

'You can take them where you like,' he replied, 'but you had better give them to the baggage-master. If you take them into the car they will draw a crowd and might get broken.'

So I gave them to the baggage-master and made haste to ask the conductor whether I might ride on the engine. He good-naturedly said: 'Yes, it's the right place for you. Run ahead, and tell the engineer what I say.' But the engineer bluntly refused to let me on, saying: 'It don't matter what the conductor told you. I say you can't ride on my engine.'

By this time the conductor, standing ready to start his train, was watching to see what luck I had, and when he saw me returning came ahead to meet me.

'The engineer won't let me on,' I reported.

'Won't he?' said the kind conductor. 'Oh! I guess he will. You come down with me.' And so he actually took the time and patience to walk the length of that long train to get me on to the engine.

'Charlie,' said he, addressing the engineer, 'don't you ever take a passenger?'

'Very seldom,' he replied.

'Anyhow, I wish you would take this young man on. He has

the strangest machines in the baggage-car I ever saw in my life. I believe he could make a locomotive. He wants to see the engine running. Let him on.' Then in a low whisper he told me to jump on, which I did gladly, the engineer offering neither encouragement nor objection.

As soon as the train was started, the engineer asked what the 'strange thing' the conductor spoke of really was.

'Only inventions for keeping time, getting folk up in the morning, and so forth,' I hastily replied, and before he could ask any more questions I asked permission to go outside of the cab to see the machinery. This he kindly granted, adding, 'Be careful not to fall off, and when you hear me whistling for a station you come back, because if it is reported against me to the superintendent that I allow boys to run all over my engine I might lose my job.'

Assuring him that I would come back promptly, I went out and walked along the foot-board on the side of the boiler, watching the magnificent machine rushing through the landscapes as if glorying in its strength like a living creature. While seated on the cow-catcher platform I seemed to be fairly flying, and the wonderful display of power and motion was enchanting. This was the first time I had ever been on a train, much less a locomotive, since I had left Scotland. When I got to Madison, I thanked the kind conductor and engineer for my glorious ride, inquired the way to the Fair, shouldered my inventions, and walked to the Fair Ground.

When I applied for an admission ticket at a window by the gate I told the agent that I had something to exhibit.

'What is it?' he inquired.

'Well, here it is. Look at it.'

When he craned his neck through the window and got a glimpse of my bundle, he cried excitedly, 'Oh! You don't need a ticket – come right in.'

When I inquired of the agent where such things as mine should be exhibited, he said, 'You see that building up on the hill with a big flag on it? That's the Fine Arts Hall, and it's just the place for your wonderful invention.'

So I went up to the Fine Arts Hall and looked in, wondering if they would allow wooden things in so fine a place.

I was met at the door by a dignified gentleman, who greeted me kindly and said, 'Young man, what have we got here?'

'Two clocks and a thermometer,' I replied.

'Did you make these? They look wonderfully beautiful and novel and must, I think, prove the most interesting feature of the fair.'

'Where shall I place them?' I inquired.

'Just look around, young man, and choose the place you like best, whether it is occupied or not. You can have your pick of all the building, and a carpenter to make the necessary shelving and assist you every way possible!'

So I quickly had a shelf made large enough for all of them, went out on the hill and picked up some glacial boulders of the right size for weights, and in fifteen or twenty minutes the clocks were running. They seemed to attract more attention than anything else in the hall. I got lots of praise from the crowd and the newspaper reporters. The local press reports were copied into the Eastern papers. It was considered wonderful that a boy on a farm had been able to invent and make such things, and almost every spectator foretold good fortune. But I had been so lectured by my father above all things to avoid praise that I was afraid to read those kind newspaper notices, and never clipped out or preserved any of them, just glanced at them and turned away my eyes from beholding vanity. They gave me a prize of ten or fifteen dollars and a diploma for wonderful things not down in the list of exhibits.

Many years later, after I had written articles and books, I received a letter from the gentleman who had charge of the Fine Arts Hall. He proved to be the Professor of English Literature in the University of Wisconsin at this Fair time, and long afterward he sent me clippings of reports of his lectures. He had a lecture on me, discussing style, et cetera, and telling how well he remembered my arrival at the Hall in my shirt-sleeves with those mechanical wonders on my shoulder, and so forth, and so forth. These inventions, though of little importance, opened all doors for me and made marks that have lasted many years, simply, I suppose, because they were original and promising.

I was looking around in the meantime to find out where I should go to seek my fortune. An inventor at the Fair, by the name of Wiard, was exhibiting an iceboat he had invented to run on the upper Mississippi from Prairie du Chien to St Paul during the winter months, explaining how useful it would be thus to make a highway of the river while it was closed to ordinary navigation by ice. After he saw my inventions he offered me a place in his foundry and machine-shop in Prairie du Chien and promised to assist me all he could. So I made up my mind to accept his offer and rode with him to Prairie du Chien in his iceboat, which was mounted on a flat car. I soon found, however, that he was seldom at home and that I was not likely to learn much at his small shop. I found a place where I could work for my board and devote my spare hours to mechanical drawing, geometry, and physics, making but little headway, however, although the Pelton family, for whom I worked, were very kind. I made up my mind after a few months' stay in Prairie du Chien to return to Madison, hoping that in some way I might be able to gain an education.

At Madison I raised a few dollars by making and selling a few of those bedsteads that set the sleepers on their feet in the morning – inserting in the footboard the works of an ordinary clock that could be bought for a dollar. I also made a few dollars addressing circulars in an insurance office, while at the same time I was paying my board by taking care of a pair of horses and going errands. This is of no great interest except that I was thus winning my bread while hoping that something would turn up that might enable me to make money enough to enter the State University. This was my ambition, and it never wavered no matter what I was doing. No University, it seemed to me, could be more admirably situated, and as I sauntered about it, charmed with its fine lawns and trees and beautiful lakes, and saw the students going and coming with their books, and occasionally practicing with a theodolite in measuring distances, I thought that if I could only join them it would be the greatest joy of life. I was desperately hungry and thirsty for knowledge and willing to endure anything to get it.

One day I chanced to meet a student who had noticed my inventions at the Fair and now recognized me. And when I said, 'You are fortunate fellows to be allowed to study in this beautiful place. I wish I could join you.' 'Well, why don't you?' he asked. 'I haven't money enough,' I said. 'Oh, as to money,' he reassuringly explained, 'very little is required. I presume you're able to enter the Freshman class, and you can board yourself as quite a number of us do at a cost of about a dollar a week. The baker and milkman come every day. You can live on bread and milk.' Well, I thought, maybe I have money enough for at least one beginning term. Anyhow I couldn't help trying.

With fear and trembling, overladen with ignorance, I called on Professor Stirling, the Dean of the Faculty, who was then Acting President, presented my case, and told him how far I had got on with my studies at home, and that I hadn't been to school since leaving Scotland at the age of eleven years, excepting one short term of a couple of months at a district school, because I could not be spared from the farm work. After hearing my story, the kind professor welcomed me to the glorious University – next, it seemed to me, to the Kingdom of Heaven. After a few weeks in the preparatory department I entered the Freshman class. In Latin I found that one of the books in use I had already studied in Scotland. So, after an interruption of a dozen years, I began my Latin over again where I had left off; and, strange to say, most of it came back to me, especially the grammar which I had committed to memory at the Dunbar Grammar School.

During the four years that I was in the University, I earned enough in the harvest-fields during the long summer vacations to carry me through the balance of each year, working very hard, cutting with a cradle four acres of wheat a day, and helping to put it in the shock. But, having to buy books and paying, I think, thirty-two dollars a year for instruction, and occasionally buying acids and retorts, glass tubing, bell-glasses, flasks, etc., I had to cut down expenses for board now and then to half a dollar a week.

One winter I taught school ten miles north of Madison, earning much-needed money at the rate of twenty dollars a month, 'boarding round,' and keeping up my University work by studying at night. As I was not then well enough off to own a watch, I used one of my hickory clocks, not only for keeping time, but for starting the school fire in the cold mornings, and regulating class-times. I carried it out on my shoulder to the old log schoolhouse, and set it to work on a little shelf nailed to one of the knotty, bulging logs. The winter was very cold, and I had to go to the schoolhouse and start the fire about eight o'clock to warm it before the arrival of the scholars. This was a rather trying job, and one that my clock might easily be made to do. Therefore, after supper one evening I told the head of the family with whom I was boarding that if he would give me a candle I would go back to the schoolhouse and make arrangements for lighting the fire at eight o'clock, without my having to be present until time to open the school at nine. He said, 'Oh, young man, you have some curious things in the school-room, but I don't think you can do that.' I said, 'Oh, yes! It's easy,' and in hardly more than an hour the simple job was completed. I had only to place a teaspoonful of powdered chlorate of potash and sugar on the stove-hearth near a few shavings and kindling, and at the required time make the clock, through a simple arrangement, touch the inflammable mixture with a drop of sulphuric acid. Every evening after school was dismissed, I shoveled out what was left of the fire into the snow, put in a little kindling, filled up the big box stove with heavy oak wood, placed the lighting arrangement on the hearth, and set the clock to drop the acid at the hour of eight; all this requiring only a few minutes.

The first morning after I had made this simple arrangement I invited the doubting farmer to watch the old squat school-house from a window that overlooked it, to see if a good smoke did not rise from the stovepipe. Sure enough, on the minute, he saw a tall column curling gracefully up through the frosty air, but instead of congratulating me on my success he solemnly shook his head and said in a hollow, lugubrious voice, 'Young man, you will be setting fire to the schoolhouse.' All winter long that faithful clock fire never failed, and by the time I got to the schoolhouse the stove was usually red-hot.

At the beginning of the long summer vacations I returned to the Hickory Hill farm to earn the means in the harvest-fields to continue my University course, walking all the way to save railroad fares. And although I cradled four acres of wheat a day, I made the long, hard, sweaty day's work still longer and harder by keeping up my study of plants. At the noon hour I collected a large handful, put them in water to keep them fresh, and after supper got to work on them and sat up till after midnight, analyzing and classifying, thus leaving only four hours for sleep; and by the end of the last year, after taking up botany, I knew the principal flowering plants of the region.

I received my first lesson in botany from a student by the name of Griswold, who is now County Judge of the County of Waukesha, Wisconsin. In the University he was often laughed at on account of his anxiety to instruct others, and his frequently saying with fine emphasis, 'Imparting instruction is my greatest enjoyment.' One memorable day in June, when I was standing on the stone steps of the north dormitory, Mr Griswold joined me and at once began to teach. He reached up, plucked a flower from an overspreading branch of a locust tree, and, handing it to me, said, 'Muir, do you know what family this tree belongs to?'

'No,' I said, 'I don't know anything about botany.'

'Well, no matter,' said he, 'what is it like?'

'It's like a pea flower,' I replied.

'That's right. You're right,' he said, 'it belongs to the Pea Family.'

'But how can that be,' I objected, 'when the pea is a weak, clinging, straggling herb, and the locust a big, thorny hardwood tree?'

'Yes, that is true,' he replied, 'as to the difference in size, but it is also true that in all their essential characters they are alike, and therefore they must belong to one and the same family. Just look at the peculiar form of the locust flower; you see that the upper petal, called the banner, is broad and erect, and so is the upper petal of the pea flower; the two lower petals, called the wings, are outspread and wing-shaped; so are those of the pea; and the two petals below the wings are united on their edges, curve upward, and form what is called the keel, and so you see are the corresponding petals of the pea flower. And now look at the stamens and pistils. You see that nine of the ten stamens have their filaments united into a sheath around the pistil, but the tenth stamen has its filament free. These are very marked characters, are they not? And, strange to say, you will find them the same in the tree and in the vine. Now look at the ovules or seeds of the locust, and you will see that they are arranged in a pod or legume like those of the pea. And look at the leaves. You see the leaf of the locust is made up of several leaflets, and so also is the leaf of the pea. Now taste the locust leaf.'

I did so and found that it tasted like the leaf of the pea. Nature has used the same seasoning for both, though one is a straggling one, the other a big tree.

'Now, surely you cannot imagine that all these similar characters are mere coincidences. Do they not rather go to show that the Creator in making the pea vine and locust tree had the same idea in mind, and that plants are not classified arbitrarily? Man has nothing to do with their classification. Nature has attended to all that, giving essential unity with boundless variety, so that the botanist has only to examine plants to learn the harmony of their relations.'

This fine lesson charmed me and sent me flying to the woods and meadows in wild enthusiasm. Like everybody else I was always fond of flowers, attracted by their external beauty and purity. Now my eyes were opened to their inner beauty, all alike revealing glorious traces of the thoughts of God, and leading on and on into the infinite cosmos. I wandered away at every opportunity, making long excursions round the lakes, gathering specimens and keeping them fresh in a bucket in my room to study at night after my regular class tasks were learned; for my eyes never closed on the plant glory I had seen.

Nevertheless, I still indulged my love of mechanical inventions. I invented a desk in which the books I had to study were arranged in order at the beginning of each term. I also made a bed which set me on my feet every morning at the hour determined on, and in dark winter mornings just as the bed set me on the floor it lighted a lamp. Then, after the minutes allowed for dressing had elapsed, a click was heard and the first book to be studied was pushed up from a rack below the top of the desk, thrown open, and allowed to remain there the number of minutes required. Then the machinery closed the book and allowed it to drop back into its stall, then moved the rack forward and threw up the next in order, and so on, all the day being divided according to the times of recitation, and time required and allotted to each study. Besides this, I thought it would be a fine thing in the summertime when the sun rose early, to dispense with the clock-controlled bed machinery, and make use of sunbeams instead. This I did simply by taking a lens out of my small spy-glass, fixing it on a frame on the sill of my bedroom window and pointing it to the sunrise; the sunbeams focused on a thread burned it through, allowing the bed machinery to put me on my feet. When I wished to arise at any given time after sunrise, I had only to turn the pivoted frame that held the lens the requisite number of degrees or minutes. Thus I took Emerson's advice and hitched my dumping-wagon bed to a star.

I also invented a machine to make visible the growth of plants and the action of the sunlight, a very delicate contrivance, enclosed in glass. Besides this I invented a barometer and a lot of novel scientific apparatus. My room was regarded as a sort of show place by the professors, who oftentimes brought visitors to it on Saturdays and holidays. And when, some eighteen years after I had left the University, I was sauntering over the campus in time of vacation, and spoke to a man who seemed to be taking some charge of the grounds, he informed me that he was the janitor; and when I inquired what had become of Pat, the janitor in my time, and a favorite with the students, he replied that Pat was still alive and well, but now too old to do much work. And when I pointed to the dormitory room that I long ago occupied, he said: 'Oh! then I know who you are,' and mentioned my name. 'How comes it that you know my name?' I inquired. He explained that 'Pat always pointed out that room to newcomers and told long stories about the wonders that used to be in it.' So long had the memory of my little inventions survived.

Although I was four years at the University, I did not take the regular course of studies, but instead picked out what I thought would be most useful to me, particularly chemistry, which opened a new world, and mathematics and physics, a little Greek and Latin, botany and geology. I was far from satisfied with what I had learned, and should have stayed longer. Anyhow I wandered away on a glorious botanical and geological excursion, which has lasted nearly fifty years and is not yet completed, always happy and free, poor and rich, without thought of a diploma or of making a name, urged on and on through endless, inspiring, Godful beauty.

From the top of a hill on the north side of Lake Mendota I gained a last wistful, lingering view of the beautiful University grounds and buildings where I had spent so many hungry and happy and hopeful days. There with streaming eyes I bade my blessed Alma Mater farewell. But I was only leaving one University for another, the Wisconsin University for the University of the Wilderness.